ALEXANDER HAMILTON

ALEXANDER HAMILTON

Steven O'Brien

CHELSEA HOUSE PUBLISHERS
NEW YORK
PHILADELPHIA

Chelsea House Publishers
EDITOR-IN-CHIEF: Nancy Toff
EXECUTIVE EDITOR: Remmel T. Nunn
MANAGING EDITOR: Karyn Gullen Browne
COPY CHIEF: Juliann Barbato
PICTURE EDITOR: Adrian G. Allen
ART DIRECTOR: Maria Epes
MANUFACTURING MANAGER: Gerald Levine

World Leaders—Past & Present
SENIOR EDITOR: John W. Selfridge

Staff for ALEXANDER HAMILTON
ASSOCIATE EDITOR: Sean Dolan
COPY EDITOR: Terrance Dolan
DEPUTY COPY CHIEF: Ellen Scordato
EDITORIAL ASSISTANT: Heather Lewis
PICTURE RESEARCHER: Andrea Reithmayer
ASSISTANT ART DIRECTOR: Laurie Jewell
DESIGNER: David Murray
PRODUCTION COORDINATOR: Joseph Romano
COVER ILLUSTRATION: Richard Martin

3 5 7 9 8 6 4

Library of Congress Cataloging in Publication Data

O'Brien, Steven.
Alexander Hamilton.

(World leaders past & present)
Bibliography: p.
Includes index.
Summary: A biography of the noted statesman and political leader
who extended many bold and creative ideas about government in the
early years of the United States.
1. Hamilton, Alexander, 1754–1804—Juvenile literature.
2. Statesmen—United States—Biography—Juvenile
literature. [1. Hamilton, Alexander, 1754–1804. 2.
Statesmen] I. Title. II. Series.
E302.6.H2024   1988   973.4′092′4 [B] [92]   87-37515

ISBN 1-55546-810-1
     0-7910-0637-9 (pbk.)

Contents

JOHN ADAMS
JOHN QUINCY ADAMS
KONRAD ADENAUER
ALEXANDER THE GREAT
SALVADOR ALLENDE
MARC ANTONY
CORAZON AQUINO
YASIR ARAFAT
KING ARTHUR
HAFEZ AL-ASSAD
KEMAL ATATÜRK
ATTILA
CLEMENT ATTLEE
AUGUSTUS CAESAR
MENACHEM BEGIN
DAVID BEN-GURION
OTTO VON BISMARCK
LÉON BLUM
SIMON BOLÍVAR
CESARE BORGIA
WILLY BRANDT
LEONID BREZHNEV
JULIUS CAESAR
JOHN CALVIN
JIMMY CARTER
FIDEL CASTRO
CATHERINE THE GREAT
CHARLEMAGNE
CHIANG KAI-SHEK
WINSTON CHURCHILL
GEORGES CLEMENCEAU
CLEOPATRA
CONSTANTINE THE GREAT
HERNÁN CORTÉS
OLIVER CROMWELL
GEORGES-JACQUES
   DANTON
JEFFERSON DAVIS
MOSHE DAYAN
CHARLES DE GAULLE
EAMON DE VALERA
EUGENE DEBS
DENG XIAOPING
BENJAMIN DISRAELI
ALEXANDER DUBČEK
FRANÇOIS & JEAN-CLAUDE
   DUVALIER
DWIGHT EISENHOWER
ELEANOR OF AQUITAINE
ELIZABETH I
FAISAL
FERDINAND & ISABELLA
FRANCISCO FRANCO
BENJAMIN FRANKLIN

FREDERICK THE GREAT
INDIRA GANDHI
MOHANDAS GANDHI
GIUSEPPE GARIBALDI
AMIN & BASHIR GEMAYEL
GENGHIS KHAN
WILLIAM GLADSTONE
MIKHAIL GORBACHEV
ULYSSES S. GRANT
ERNESTO "CHE" GUEVARA
TENZIN GYATSO
ALEXANDER HAMILTON
DAG HAMMARSKJÖLD
HENRY VIII
HENRY OF NAVARRE
PAUL VON HINDENBURG
HIROHITO
ADOLF HITLER
HO CHI MINH
KING HUSSEIN
IVAN THE TERRIBLE
ANDREW JACKSON
JAMES I
WOJCIECH JARUZELSKI
THOMAS JEFFERSON
JOAN OF ARC
POPE JOHN XXIII
POPE JOHN PAUL II
LYNDON JOHNSON
BENITO JUÁREZ
JOHN KENNEDY
ROBERT KENNEDY
JOMO KENYATTA
AYATOLLAH KHOMEINI
NIKITA KHRUSHCHEV
KIM IL SUNG
MARTIN LUTHER KING, JR.
HENRY KISSINGER
KUBLAI KHAN
LAFAYETTE
ROBERT E. LEE
VLADIMIR LENIN
ABRAHAM LINCOLN
DAVID LLOYD GEORGE
LOUIS XIV
MARTIN LUTHER
JUDAS MACCABEUS
JAMES MADISON
NELSON & WINNIE
   MANDELA
MAO ZEDONG
FERDINAND MARCOS
GEORGE MARSHALL

MARY, QUEEN OF SCOTS
TOMÁŠ MASARYK
GOLDA MEIR
KLEMENS VON METTERNICH
JAMES MONROE
HOSNI MUBARAK
ROBERT MUGABE
BENITO MUSSOLINI
NAPOLÉON BONAPARTE
GAMAL ABDEL NASSER
JAWAHARLAL NEHRU
NERO
NICHOLAS II
RICHARD NIXON
KWAME NKRUMAH
DANIEL ORTEGA
MOHAMMED REZA PAHLAVI
THOMAS PAINE
CHARLES STEWART
   PARNELL
PERICLES
JUAN PERÓN
PETER THE GREAT
POL POT
MUAMMAR EL-QADDAFI
RONALD REAGAN
CARDINAL RICHELIEU
MAXIMILIEN ROBESPIERRE
ELEANOR ROOSEVELT
FRANKLIN ROOSEVELT
THEODORE ROOSEVELT
ANWAR SADAT
HAILE SELASSIE
PRINCE SIHANOUK
JAN SMUTS
JOSEPH STALIN
SUKARNO
SUN YAT-SEN
TAMERLANE
MOTHER TERESA
MARGARET THATCHER
JOSIP BROZ TITO
TOUSSAINT L'OUVERTURE
LEON TROTSKY
PIERRE TRUDEAU
HARRY TRUMAN
QUEEN VICTORIA
LECH WALESA
GEORGE WASHINGTON
CHAIM WEIZMANN
WOODROW WILSON
XERXES
EMILIANO ZAPATA
ZHOU ENLAI

CHELSEA HOUSE PUBLISHERS

ON LEADERSHIP

Arthur M. Schlesinger, jr.

LEADERSHIP, it may be said, is really what makes the world go round. Love no doubt smooths the passage; but love is a private transaction between consenting adults. Leadership is a public transaction with history. The idea of leadership affirms the capacity of individuals to move, inspire, and mobilize masses of people so that they act together in pursuit of an end. Sometimes leadership serves good purposes, sometimes bad; but whether the end is benign or evil, great leaders are those men and women who leave their personal stamp on history.

Now, the very concept of leadership implies the proposition that individuals can make a difference. This proposition has never been universally accepted. From classical times to the present day, eminent thinkers have regarded individuals as no more than the agents and pawns of larger forces, whether the gods and goddesses of the ancient world or, in the modern era, race, class, nation, the dialectic, the will of the people, the spirit of the times, history itself. Against such forces, the individual dwindles into insignificance.

So contends the thesis of historical determinism. Tolstoy's great novel *War and Peace* offers a famous statement of the case. Why, Tolstoy asked, did millions of men in the Napoleonic Wars, denying their human feelings and their common sense, move back and forth across Europe slaughtering their fellows? "The war," Tolstoy answered, "was bound to happen simply because it was bound to happen." All prior history predetermined it. As for leaders, they, Tolstoy said, "are but the labels that serve to give a name to an end and, like labels, they have the least possible connection with the event." The greater the leader, "the more conspicuous the inevitability and the predestination of every act he commits." The leader, said Tolstoy, is "the slave of history."

Determinism takes many forms. Marxism is the determinism of class. Nazism the determinism of race. But the idea of men and women as the slaves of history runs athwart the deepest human instincts. Rigid determinism abolishes the idea of human freedom—

the assumption of free choice that underlies every move we make, every word we speak, every thought we think. It abolishes the idea of human responsibility, since it is manifestly unfair to reward or punish people for actions that are by definition beyond their control. No one can live consistently by any deterministic creed. The Marxist states prove this themselves by their extreme susceptibility to the cult of leadership.

More than that, history refutes the idea that individuals make no difference. In December 1931 a British politician crossing Park Avenue in New York City between 76th and 77th Streets around 10:30 P.M. looked in the wrong direction and was knocked down by an automobile—a moment, he later recalled, of a man aghast, a world aglare: "I do not understand why I was not broken like an eggshell or squashed like a gooseberry." Fourteen months later an American politician, sitting in an open car in Miami, Florida, was fired on by an assassin; the man beside him was hit. Those who believe that individuals make no difference to history might well ponder whether the next two decades would have been the same had Mario Constasino's car killed Winston Churchill in 1931 and Giuseppe Zangara's bullet killed Franklin Roosevelt in 1933. Suppose, in addition, that Adolf Hitler had been killed in the street fighting during the Munich *Putsch* of 1923 and that Lenin had died of typhus during World War I. What would the 20th century be like now?

For better or for worse, individuals do make a difference. "The notion that a people can run itself and its affairs anonymously," wrote the philosopher William James, "is now well known to be the silliest of absurdities. Mankind does nothing save through initiatives on the part of inventors, great or small, and imitation by the rest of us—these are the sole factors in human progress. Individuals of genius show the way, and set the patterns, which common people then adopt and follow."

Leadership, James suggests, means leadership in thought as well as in action. In the long run, leaders in thought may well make the greater difference to the world. But, as Woodrow Wilson once said, "Those only are leaders of men, in the general eye, who lead in action. . . . It is at their hands that new thought gets its translation into the crude language of deeds." Leaders in thought often invent in solitude and obscurity, leaving to later generations the tasks of imitation. Leaders in action—the leaders portrayed in this series—have to be effective in their own time.

And they cannot be effective by themselves. They must act in response to the rhythms of their age. Their genius must be adapted, in a phrase of William James's, "to the receptivities of the moment." Leaders are useless without followers. "There goes the mob," said the French politician hearing a clamor in the streets. "I am their leader. I must follow them." Great leaders turn the inchoate emotions of the mob to purposes of their own. They seize on the opportunities of their time, the hopes, fears, frustrations, crises, potentialities. They succeed when events have prepared the way for them, when the community is awaiting to be aroused, when they can provide the clarifying and organizing ideas. Leadership ignites the circuit between the individual and the mass and thereby alters history.

It may alter history for better or for worse. Leaders have been responsible for the most extravagant follies and most monstrous crimes that have beset suffering humanity. They have also been vital in such gains as humanity has made in individual freedom, religious and racial tolerance, social justice, and respect for human rights.

There is no sure way to tell in advance who is going to lead for good and who for evil. But a glance at the gallery of men and women in *World Leaders—Past and Present* suggests some useful tests.

One test is this: Do leaders lead by force or by persuasion? By command or by consent? Through most of history leadership was exercised by the divine right of authority. The duty of followers was to defer and to obey. "Theirs not to reason why / Theirs but to do and die." On occasion, as with the so-called enlightened despots of the 18th century in Europe, absolutist leadership was animated by humane purposes. More often, absolutism nourished the passion for domination, land, gold, and conquest and resulted in tyranny.

The great revolution of modern times has been the revolution of equality. The idea that all people should be equal in their legal condition has undermined the old structure of authority, hierarchy, and deference. The revolution of equality has had two contrary effects on the nature of leadership. For equality, as Alexis de Tocqueville pointed out in his great study *Democracy in America*, might mean equality in servitude as well as equality in freedom.

"I know of only two methods of establishing equality in the political world," Tocqueville wrote. "Rights must be given to every citizen, or none at all to anyone . . . save one, who is the master of all." There was no middle ground "between the sovereignty of all and the absolute power of one man." In his astonishing prediction of 20th-century totalitarian dictatorship, Tocqueville explained how the revolution of equality could lead to the *"Führerprinzip"* and more terrible absolutism than the world had ever known.

But when rights are given to every citizen and the sovereignty of all is established, the problem of leadership takes a new form, becomes more exacting than ever before. It is easy to issue commands and enforce them by the rope and the stake, the concentration camp and the *gulag.* It is much harder to use argument and achievement to overcome opposition and win consent. The Founding Fathers of the United States understood the difficulty. They believed that history had given them the opportunity to decide, as Alexander Hamilton wrote in the first Federalist Paper, whether men are indeed capable of basing government on "reflection and choice, or whether they are forever destined to depend . . . on accident and force."

Government by reflection and choice called for a new style of leadership and a new quality of followership. It required leaders to be responsive to popular concerns, and it required followers to be active and informed participants in the process. Democracy does not eliminate emotion from politics; sometimes it fosters demagoguery; but it is confident that, as the greatest of democratic leaders put it, you cannot fool all of the people all of the time. It measures leadership by results and retires those who overreach or falter or fail.

It is true that in the long run despots are measured by results too. But they can postpone the day of judgment, sometimes indefinitely, and in the meantime they can do infinite harm. It is also true that democracy is no guarantee of virtue and intelligence in government, for the voice of the people is not necessarily the voice of God. But democracy, by assuring the right of opposition, offers built-in resistance to the evils inherent in absolutism. As the theologian Reinhold Niebuhr summed it up, "Man's capacity for justice makes democracy possible, but man's inclination to injustice makes democracy necessary."

A second test for leadership is the end for which power is sought. When leaders have as their goal the supremacy of a master race or the promotion of totalitarian revolution or the acquisition and exploitation of colonies or the protection of greed and privilege or the preservation of personal power, it is likely that their leadership will do little to advance the cause of humanity. When their goal is the abolition of slavery, the liberation of women, the enlargement of opportunity for the poor and powerless, the extension of equal rights to racial minorities, the defense of the freedoms of expression and opposition, it is likely that their leadership will increase the sum of human liberty and welfare.

Leaders have done great harm to the world. They have also conferred great benefits. You will find both sorts in this series. Even "good" leaders must be regarded with a certain wariness. Leaders are not demigods; they put on their trousers one leg after another just like ordinary mortals. No leader is infallible, and every leader needs to be reminded of this at regular intervals. Irreverence irritates leaders but is their salvation. Unquestioning submission corrupts leaders and demeans followers. Making a cult of a leader is always a mistake. Fortunately hero worship generates its own antidote. "Every hero," said Emerson, "becomes a bore at last."

The signal benefit the great leaders confer is to embolden the rest of us to live according to our own best selves, to be active, insistent, and resolute in affirming our own sense of things. For great leaders attest to the reality of human freedom against the supposed inevitabilities of history. And they attest to the wisdom and power that may lie within the most unlikely of us, which is why Abraham Lincoln remains the supreme example of great leadership. A great leader, said Emerson, exhibits new possibilities to all humanity. "We feed on genius. . . . Great men exist that there may be greater men."

Great leaders, in short, justify themselves by emancipating and empowering their followers. So humanity struggles to master its destiny, remembering with Alexis de Tocqueville: "It is true that around every man a fatal circle is traced beyond which he cannot pass; but within the wide verge of that circle he is powerful and free; as it is with man, so with communities."

1

Duel at Weehawken

Shortly before dawn on Wednesday, July 11, 1804, Alexander Hamilton, his second, Nathaniel Pendleton, and his personal physician, Dr. David Hosack, embarked in a small boat from New York City on a three-mile journey across the Hudson River to Weehawken, New Jersey. It was a warm summer morning. As their boat reached the New Jersey shore a gentle breeze blew away the last lingering wisps of morning mist.

Aaron Burr and his second, William P. Van Ness, were waiting at Weehawken when Hamilton and his party arrived. Events proceeded according to the strict code of etiquette — the *code duello* — governing such encounters between gentlemen. After Hamilton and Burr formally greeted each other, their seconds drew lots to determine where each combatant would stand and which second would announce the rules of the engagement. Pendleton won both draws and carefully explained that once the antagonists were standing at their marked positions 10 yards apart he would say, "Pre-sent!" This was the signal for the participants to raise their pistols, take aim, and fire. If one shot before the other, the opposite second would count aloud, "One, two, three, fire!" That duelist then had to shoot or lose his turn.

> *[Hamilton] allowed himself to be drawn into a duel but instead of killing Burr, he invited Burr to kill him.*
> —HENRY ADAMS
> historian

The site above the Hudson River at Weehawken, New Jersey, where Aaron Burr fatally wounded Alexander Hamilton in a duel on July 11, 1804. Vice-president Burr fled resulting murder indictments in New York and New Jersey and returned to Washington, D.C., where he presided over the impeachment of Supreme Court Justice Samuel Chase.

13

Accompanied by their seconds, Nathaniel Pendleton and William Van Ness, Hamilton (left) and Burr (right) prepare to fire upon one another. Hamilton believed that to refuse Burr's challenge to duel would ruin any chance of resuming his political career.

Hamilton opposed dueling and had decided he would not fire at Burr. He would let Burr shoot first and then fire his pistol into the air.

Hamilton and Burr assumed their positions. As Pendleton repeated his explanation of the commands, Hamilton practiced lifting and looking down the barrel of his weapon. He then put on a pair of glasses. "I beg pardon for delaying you," he said to Burr, "but the direction of the light renders it necessary."

As soon as Hamilton was ready, Pendleton cried, "Pre-sent!" Both men leveled their pistols and took careful aim. Burr fired first. His bullet entered Hamilton's right side and shattered his spinal column. Hamilton fired his pistol in a reflex action and collapsed. Pendleton and Dr. Hosack rushed to Hamilton's side to treat his wound, but Hamilton accurately assessed his own condition: "This is a mortal wound Doctor . . . Pendleton knows . . . I did not intend to fire at him."

Alexander Hamilton was born on Nevis, a small island in the Caribbean Sea that is part of the archipelago known then as the British West Indies. Much about Hamilton's early life remains obscure. Even the year of his birth is open to question. Many historians now believe that he was born on January 11, 1755, although Hamilton himself hinted that he was born two years later. His mother, Rachel Faucett (her family name is also given as Fawcette, Faucette, Faucitt, and other variations), was the daughter of a fairly well-off French Huguenot (Protestant) planter and physician. Her parents' marriage was an unhappy one, and eventually they separated. Rachel, by this time an extremely independent and strong-willed young woman, accompanied her mother to the Danish island of St. Croix. There she met John Lavien (again, the name has been given several ways, including Levine and Lavine) and, possibly at the encouragement of her mother, married him, probably in the mid-1740s. The Faucetts believed Lavien to be wealthy, but he had enjoyed little success as a planter and was actually considerably in debt. Other factors weighed against the likelihood of a successful marriage. For one, Rachel was young — most likely still in her teens — and high-spirited, whereas Lavien was middle-aged. In 1750 Lavien had his young wife imprisoned for "indecent and very suspicious behavior," meaning adultery.

Lavien had hoped that a show of power would tame his young wife's rebellious spirit, but he could not have been more mistaken. Upon her release she fled St. Croix, abandoning her young son, Peter, as well as her husband. Some time in the next few years she took up with James Hamilton, the fourth son of a Scottish nobleman, with whom she settled on Nevis. Like many other Europeans in the 18th century, James Hamilton had come to the West Indies to make his fortune. The sugar trade provided the most common way to riches. With the European nations craving "white gold" and imported African slave labor readily available, it was possible to turn a comparatively small amount of capital into enormous wealth. However, in the highly speculative

Hamilton's silence about his mother was matched by the empty formality of his infrequent references to his father.
—JACOB E. COOKE
Hamilton biographer

Under watchful eyes, slaves cut sugarcane, the main cash crop of the West Indies. Plantation owners in the Caribbean depended entirely upon slave labor to work their fields. Hamilton's mother owned slaves, but her son became active in New York's antislavery movement.

economic environment of the British West Indies there were more than a few failures, and James Hamilton was destined to be among that number. Whatever money he may have had upon arrival he soon squandered on pleasurable pursuits and ill-fated business ventures.

James Hamilton had problems besides his financial woes. He and Rachel had two sons — James, probably born in 1753, and Alexander. John Lavien obtained a divorce decree in 1759; under its terms Rachel was forbidden to remarry. James Hamilton tried to make a go of family life for several more years, until late 1765 or early 1766, when he left his wife and children on St. Croix, never to return.

As an adult Hamilton seldom spoke of his parents, although he referred more frequently to his father than to his mother. It appears that Hamilton never held his father's fecklessness against him, and in later life the two resumed communications, although their relationship consisted of only a half dozen stilted letters. The fact that Hamilton was an illegitimate child would eventually be a source of some embarrassment for him, but he remained proud of his father's noble bloodlines.

After her lover's desertion, Rachel had little immediate choice but to depend on the generosity of St. Croix relatives for survival. The family settled in Christiansted, whose 800 white residents made it the island's largest city. (On all of St. Croix there were only 2,000 whites; black slaves outnumbered the white population by a ratio of approximately 12 to 1.) After a short time she was able to rent a small house, in which she opened a general store. She also earned money by renting out slaves she had inherited from her mother. Both children helped out in the store, although James soon found other work as a carpenter's apprentice and Alexander took a job with the trading firm of Beckman and Cruger. Though the family was poor, Rachel was able to indulge her love of literature by purchasing 34 books. Alexander had little formal schooling; the many hours he spent with his mother's books constituted the most important part of his early education.

Rachel Hamilton died in February 1768 of a tropical fever. The few effects of her estate were claimed by John Lavien on behalf of her legitimate son, Peter. Care of the Hamilton children fell to her brother-in-law, Peter Lytton, but the following year he committed suicide. It is believed Hamilton was taken in by a friend's family.

By this time Hamilton had already demonstrated a head for figures, and his obvious intelligence convinced Nicholas Cruger, head of the trading firm where Hamilton was employed, to give him increased responsibility. Even so, the extremely ambitious and confident Hamilton felt constrained by his circumstances. In a 1769 letter to his friend Edward Stevens, who was then at King's College (later Columbia University) in New York City, Hamilton wrote, "I contemn the grov'ling condition of a clerk or the like, to which my fortune, etc. condemns me and would willingly risk my life tho' not my character to exalt my Station." Shrewdly aware of the need to secure financial assistance to escape his impoverished condition and confident of his ability to accomplish any task given him, Hamilton concentrated all his considerable talents on making the most of any opportunities for improvement that crossed his path. When Cruger went to New York City 2 years later, he left the 16-year-old Hamilton in charge of the business while he was away.

A tropical storm proved to be young Hamilton's ticket to a new life. When St. Croix was battered by a devastating hurricane in 1772, Hamilton wrote a vivid account of what occurred. In the style of the

Hamilton was born in this house on the West Indian island of Nevis, probably in 1755. Historians have speculated that Hamilton's illegitimacy made him especially determined to succeed.

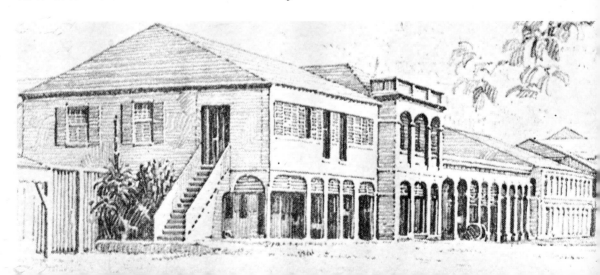

Hamilton sat for this drawing on his 18th birthday, January 11, 1773. By this time he had left the West Indies and was enrolled in preparatory school in Elizabethtown, New Jersey.

day, his impassioned prose was concerned less with realistic description than with focusing on the hurricane as a demonstration of God's power and man's comparative frailty. When he showed it to the Reverend Hugh Knox, a Presbyterian clergyman who had been tutoring the talented youth, Knox was so impressed that he had it published in the island's newspaper. (That same journal had earlier published two love poems and an essay on governmental theory by Hamilton.)

The hurricane article attracted much favorable attention and gave impetus to a plan Knox had to send Hamilton to college in the British colonies in North America. Cruger had been thinking similarly for some time and was willing to help finance the project. The two men also obtained help from other aristocratic islanders impressed with Hamilton, and in October 1772 the young clerk embarked for Boston, in the Massachusetts colony.

After only a brief stay in Boston, Hamilton made his way to New York City, preceded by letters of introduction from Cruger and Knox to clergymen and some of the city's leading citizens. The correspondence avoided detailed explanations of Hamilton's background, and his illegitimacy seems not to have hindered his social acceptance. Hamilton was careful to curry favor among the influential New York and New Jersey families he was introduced to. They described him as a cheerful, attractive young man of sound character and good study habits.

Hamilton entered King's College (now Columbia University) in New York in the fall of 1773. Allowed to proceed at his own lively pace, he completed his studies there two and a half years later, shortly before the college closed due to the outbreak of the revolutionary war.

Knox's plan called for Hamilton to enroll at the College of New Jersey (later Princeton University), but before he could do so he required preliminary work to prepare himself for the school's rigorous curriculum, which included English literature, composition, mathematics, geography, public speaking, Greek, Latin, and French. Hamilton was accepted as a student at a preparatory school in Elizabethtown, New Jersey, where he was allowed to work at his own pace, and he mastered his studies within a year. When the College of New Jersey's president, John Witherspoon, would not permit Hamilton a similar arrangement at his school, he applied instead for admission to King's College, which was quick to accept him. Permitted once again to advance as rapidly as his abilities allowed, Hamilton received private instruction from the university's president and instructors and raced

On December 16, 1773, Bostonians opposed to British taxation disguised themselves as Indians, boarded British merchant ships anchored in Boston Harbor, and dumped hundreds of pounds of tea overboard in what became known as the Boston Tea Party. Britain's harsh retaliatory measures aroused further colonial resistance and led to the calling of the First Continental Congress.

The title page from the first edition of Hamilton's *A Full Vindication of the Measures of the Congress*, his 1774 response to the pseudonymous Westchester Farmer, who had criticized the Continental Congress. The 19-year-old Hamilton was an enthusiastic supporter of opposition to Great Britain.

through the school's requirements in two and a half years, although he never took a formal degree.

Hamilton had come to the colonies during turbulent times. Hard-pressed financially because of expenses incurred in extending and defending its vast overseas empire, Great Britain eyed the economically prosperous North American colonies as a source of revenue. Beginning in the 1760s, Britain's Parliament imposed a series of taxes on various items in the colonies, including the stamps needed for most official and other printed documents, paint, paper, glass, and such imported staples as sugar and tea. Like most Englishmen, the colonists were proud of Britain's system of representative government, as manifested in the right to elect delegates to Parliament, which in turn had the right to legislate for the nation. The governments of the 13 colonies had been established upon the same theory of representative government. However, the stamp, tea, and other taxes had been imposed not by the elected colonial assemblies but by the British Parliament, in which the colonists were not represented. To the colonists, such taxation without representation smacked of tyranny. Opposition to the acts was widespread and sometimes violent. Britain responded by sending troops to Boston, the center of dissent, in 1770. In May 1773 Parliament passed a new tea act, which maintained the tea tax and granted a British company a monopoly on its importation. That December, colonists, many of them dressed like Indians, boarded British merchant ships in Boston Harbor and threw cartons of tea overboard. Britain responded to the Boston Tea Party by issuing what became known as the Intolerable Acts. The legislation closed Boston's port to shipping, suspended local government in Massachusetts, and required the quartering of British troops within the city.

Although a newcomer, Hamilton did not hesitate to take sides. He may have written articles in New York newspapers defending the destruction of the taxed tea, although, in the style of the day, the articles were published under a pseudonym, and definitive authorship has not been established. According to his grandson, in July of 1774 Hamilton gave a fiery speech at the Fields (now City Hall Park) in lower Manhattan, urging the colonies to unite in resistance to British oppression.

Alarmed by the severity of the British treatment of Massachusetts, representatives from 12 of the colonies — Georgia did not send a delegation — convened the First Continental Congress at Philadelphia in September 1774. The Congress agreed on a program of outright resistance to the Intolerable Acts, with a boycott on all trade with Britain and its other colonies as the cornerstone of its strategy.

The outbreak of the revolutionary war seemed to afford Hamilton the opportunity for military glory he had long coveted. He joined the Continental Army as an artillery captain in March 1776. Although he distinguished himself on Washington's retreat across New Jersey, the heroism he sought eluded him.

The revolutionary war began on April 19, 1775, when British troops fired upon armed colonial militiamen on the town common of Lexington, Massachusetts. After further hostilities at the neighboring village of Concord, the redcoats retreated under withering fire from colonists hidden behind stone walls along the main road to Boston.

Not all the colonists supported the Continental Congress. One who did not was the Reverend Samuel Seabury, an Episcopal clergyman who published a number of attacks on the Continental Congress under the pen name "A Westchester Farmer." In response Hamilton wrote an essay entitled *A Full Vindication of the Measures of the Congress*, which appeared in December 1774, and a longer and more sophisticated sequel, *The Farmer Refuted*, which appeared several months later. In them he argued for the equality of all men, the natural right of people to freedom and happiness, the danger of giving unregulated power to government officials or institutions, and the right of citizens to resort to arms if necessary to overthrow tyranny. The Intolerable Acts, he asserted, must be resisted, preferably by adherence to Congress's economic boycott, but even by war should Britain press the issue. When Hamilton's authorship became known — the articles had been published anonymously — there was general amazement that the writer of such sophisticated polemics was so young.

Six years earlier, in the same letter to Edward Stevens in which he had lamented his lowly station in life, Hamilton had confessed that he wished there would be a war, for a war would provide him with the opportunity for glory that he coveted. The conflict between the colonies and Britain seemed destined to give him his opportunity. Fighting between American militiamen and British soldiers broke out at the Massachusetts towns of Lexington and Concord in April 1775. For some time prior to the outbreak of hostilities Hamilton had been drilling with a volunteer militia group in New York City. Despite his allegiance to the rebels, Hamilton opposed the acts of violence that were directed against Loyalists, or Tories, as they were known. There were, he declared, wise and good men on both sides of the issue, and he could not "presume to think every man who differs from him either a fool or knave." When an angry mob attacked the home of Myles Cooper, the Tory president of King's College, Hamilton helped him escape. In a letter to John Jay, a New York delegate to the Continental Congress, Hamilton denounced such activity as particularly dangerous "in times of such commotion as the present," when "the passions of men are worked up to an uncommon pitch." For Hamilton, revolution did not mean anarchy. Like other exponents of the revolutionary cause, such as Thomas Jefferson, Hamilton argued that the justification for the colonists' rebellion against Britain lay in the mother country's violation of a universal system of natural rights and laws regulating the relationship between individuals and their government. From Hamilton's viewpoint, it was important to guarantee that the coming of war did not mean an end to the rule of law. If left unchecked, he warned, "the same state of the passions which fits the multitude . . . for opposition to tyranny and oppression, very naturally leads them to a contempt and disregard of all authority."

Thanks to his friends in the Continental Congress, in March 1776 Hamilton secured an appointment as a captain of artillery. Certain that he was destined to be remembered for his exploits in battle, Hamilton was eager to prove his mettle.

> On the evening of May 10, 1775, a "murderous band" of about four hundred men had gathered to attack the home of the King's College president. To Hamilton that was simply not acceptable: preparing to fight a war for American liberty was one thing, wantonly destroying the property and imperiling the life of a defenseless individual, however odious his opinions, was quite another.
> —FORREST McDONALD
> Hamilton biographer

2

The Revolution

Hamilton did not have to wait long to demonstrate his courage. The British general Sir William Howe, supported by a large fleet and in command of 32,000 men, defeated the American army at the Battle of Long Island in August 1776 and drove it from Manhattan a few weeks later. George Washington, the American commander, was forced to take the remnants of his army north, where he was again defeated by Howe, this time at White Plains, and then southwestward across New Jersey into Pennsylvania. Undaunted by the collapse of his inexperienced militia when confronted by British regulars, Washington led his men across the frozen Delaware River on Christmas night and surprised the predominantly Hessian (German mercenary) troops at Trenton, New Jersey. He took more than 900 prisoners, and his own forces suffered only 4 casualties.

Hamilton and his artillery company distinguished themselves on the retreat through New Jersey and at the battles of Trenton and Princeton. The valor and composure of the young officer did not go unnoticed by his colleagues, who dubbed him the Little Lion. When the exhausted American forces settled

There is a certain enthusiasm in liberty, that makes human nature rise above itself, in acts of bravery and heroism.
—ALEXANDER HAMILTON

Shown here in a painting by the American portrait artist Charles Willson Peale, Hamilton made his greatest contribution to the revolutionary war effort as an aide to General George Washington. He earned the rank of lieutenant colonel yet was frustrated by Washington's unwillingness to give him a command of his own.

Washington accepts the surrender of the Hessians (German soldiers employed by Great Britain) at the Battle of Trenton. The American forces crossed the ice-clogged Delaware River on Christmas night and surprised the British and German troops in their barracks early the following morning.

into winter quarters at Morristown, New Jersey, two major generals asked Hamilton to serve as their aide-de-camp, but he declined out of distaste for the "kind of personal dependence" the position would entail and the hope that he would be offered a command of his own. But when Washington asked him to join his staff and offered a promotion to lieutenant colonel as part of the bargain, Hamilton could not refuse.

Washington knew that dislodging the British from America was going to require the creation of a military organization that could manage a long continental war and the transformation of what was essentially an amalgamation of local militias into a professional army. The military staff he assembled to achieve these goals included some of the most talented and best educated men in America.

Although twice Hamilton's age and from a completely different background, the aristocratic middle-aged Virginian established an extremely productive and creative working relationship with the illegitimate 22-year-old from the West Indies. Washington's renowned self-control and patience helped steady the proud, sensitive Hamilton, who had a tendency to lash out at all perceived affronts.

Faced with the responsibility of corresponding with and placating an anxious Congress, the various state governments, and the new nation's prospective allies, as well as commanding his fighting forces, Washington had little choice but to delegate a great deal of these tasks among his 32 talented aides. Foremost among an aide's duties was correspondence. Washington did not expect his assistants to be knowledgeable about military strategy, asking only that they "write a good letter, write quick, are methodical, and diligent."

With little time for dictation, Washington usually provided only general instructions and relied on the ability and initiative of his assistants for the successful completion of all necessary correspondence. Hamilton could do this so well that he was referred to as "the pen for the army," and headquarters staff came to treat orders or advice from Hamilton with the same respect and obedience as Washington's. Hamilton's fluency in French proved to be critically important, as Washington spent much time writing to French diplomats and ministers, attempting to woo France into a treaty of alliance with the newly united states. Although the bulk of his duties consisted of letter writing, Hamilton also drafted plans for the reorganization of the army and the inspector general's office, wrote a new set of military regulations, compiled intelligence reports, and carried out special military and diplomatic missions.

Washington confers with Hamilton. Washington's aides were an extremely talented group; none was more indispensable to the commander in chief than Hamilton. His abilities were so great that Washington was reluctant to release him to the command he so coveted.

Peale's portrait of Hamilton's close friend John Laurens of South Carolina. Educated in Europe, Laurens also served as Washington's aide before resigning to form battalions of freed slaves to fight for the revolutionary cause.

Most of Washington's aides were, like Hamilton, bachelors in their twenties. Among themselves, Washington's staff referred to their close-knit and harmonious group as "the family," and Hamilton was accepted as a full-fledged member. It was during this time that Hamilton formed a deep friendship with John Laurens, a South Carolinian and fellow aide. Although Hamilton possessed abundant charm, it served as a veneer for an essential reserve that permitted him to make few lasting or intimate friendships.

Service as Washington's aide gave Hamilton the opportunity to mingle regularly with the American aristocracy, one of whom, General Philip Schuyler, an extremely wealthy landowner, was impressed enough by Hamilton's brilliance and appeal to allow him to court his daughter, Elizabeth. The two met in November 1779. Nearly three years younger than Hamilton, Elizabeth had, Hamilton confided to a friend, fine dark eyes, a pretty face, masses of dark hair, and a sweet disposition. She, in turn, might have described him as a thin man of average height with small shoulders and a high forehead, who liked to wear his powdered reddish brown hair pulled tightly back from his face. In an earlier letter to Laurens, Hamilton had commented on the qualifications his ideal wife should possess: "As to fortune, the larger stock of that the better . . . as I have not much of my own." Although Hamilton undoubtedly benefited by his connection with the prestigious Schuyler family, his letters to Elizabeth and future devotion demonstrate that the romance was a love match. They were married on December 14, 1780, in the Schuyler home in Albany, New York.

In addition to his heavy work load for Washington, Hamilton carried on an extensive personal correspondence with powerful American political and financial leaders. Most of these letters concerned his ideas for shaping America's future and prefigured the theories he would later put into practice. The most important missives were written during a period when Hamilton had grown disillusioned with the war effort, with what he viewed as his own lack of achievement, and with the nation's government.

At the time the American army was undermanned and undersupplied. It was not long after the difficult winter at Valley Forge, Pennsylvania, when many soldiers had died from sickness and cold. There was much squabbling and intrigue among the officers, and one commander, Horatio Gates, who received public credit for the critical American victory at Saratoga, New York, was even scheming to get himself named to replace Washington. Major General Benedict Arnold, the true hero of Saratoga, committed treason by conspiring to surrender the fort at West Point, New York, to the British. Congress was essentially without funds, the states were reluctant to contribute more, and the new currency that had been issued lacked the public's confidence and was rapidly losing value.

As Hamilton saw it, the chief problems were sectionalism and a weak central government. Unaccustomed to thinking in a national sense, many Americans thought in terms of what would benefit their region and state rather than the nation as a whole. As several biographers have pointed out, Hamilton, being from the West Indies, had no such sectional loyalties. From the outset his outlook was distinctly national. For Hamilton, however, the problem of sectionalism was secondary to the creation of a strong central government. Having rebelled against the oppressive authority of the British king and Parliament, the American people were extremely wary of granting too much power to their new governmental institutions. Thus, the Congress was dependent upon the individual states to provide it with funds and could not impose taxes to raise revenues. It could enact legislation but had no power to enforce it, and it could not regulate trade. With the ratification of the Articles of Confederation in February 1781, these shortcomings, confirmed in practice, were codified as the law of the land.

Hamilton railed against this "fundamental defect" in his letters. Congress could never be expected to conduct the war properly so long as it was dependent upon the states to fund it and enforce its will. The Articles of Confederation proclaimed that each

Philip Schuyler was one of the wealthiest landowners in New York State. Hamilton, who had neither money nor a prominent family name, had little to recommend him as a suitor for Schuyler's daughter. Nonetheless, Schuyler believed Hamilton had a bright future and did not discourage their courtship.

Elizabeth Schuyler married Alexander Hamilton in Albany, New York, on December 14, 1780. Elizabeth was not as beautiful or outgoing as her older sister, Angelica, but her lovely dark eyes won her many admirers, including Hamilton.

state was to retain its "sovereignty, freedom and independence, and every power, jurisdiction and right" that was not expressly delegated to Congress — a position Hamilton diametrically opposed. The states, he argued, must surrender some of their sovereignty to a federal body in order to form a stronger union. This central authority should possess all of the powers necessary to meet whatever national needs should arise; it, not the states, would have the right to exercise all those powers not expressly delegated. Furthermore, the central government should possess an executive branch as well as a legislative body. The establishment of a strong central government would make possible the economic reforms Hamilton regarded as essential, including the creation of a national bank.

Hamilton began to chafe at the restrictions inherent in his position as an aide, believing that his talents enabled him to do much more. He again clamored for a command of his own. Influential friends such as Laurens, the Marquis de Lafayette, and Nathanael Greene recommended Hamilton for important posts, but Washington refused, believing that Hamilton was irreplaceable where he was. In February 1781 Hamilton's frustration caused him to boil over. Informed by Washington that his presence was required, Hamilton asked the general's leave to deliver an important message to another room at headquarters, then dallied briefly on his return to converse with Lafayette. Washington was short-tempered that day; he chastised Hamilton, telling him, "You have kept me waiting at the head of the stairs these ten minutes. I must tell you Sir you treat me with disrespect." Hamilton replied, "I am not conscious of it Sir, but since you have thought it necessary to tell me so we part."

Although Washington quickly apologized, Hamilton pouted. The general had a genuine fondness for Hamilton as well as a need for his talents, but Hamilton refused to take back his resignation and agreed only to stay on until Washington found an adequate replacement. Although the two repaired their working relationship, there is evidence that Hamilton never returned the affection Washington demonstrated for him. In a letter to his father-in-law written shortly after the incident, Hamilton said of Washington that "for three years past I have felt no friendship for him and have professed none," adding that he served the general because "his popularity has often been essential to the safety of America, and is still of great importance to it." Although Hamilton may have written this out of anger, his future correspondence with Washington was noticeably free of the endearments and other evidence of personal feeling found in Washington's letters.

Determined now to obtain reassignment, Hamilton ultimately had to threaten to resign his commission to receive his wish. On July 31, 1781, he was given command of a New York light infantry battalion. The appointment came in time for him to take part in the American attack on the British-held fort at Yorktown, Virginia. Hamilton led an attack on a fortified position that succeeded in forcing the British to fall back, but his battalion did not play a crucial role in the battle. Aided by French land and naval forces, the Americans forced the British to surrender, bringing the revolutionary war to an end.

Washington and the Marquis de Lafayette, a Frenchman who served as a general with the American forces during the revolutionary war, review the freezing American troops at Valley Forge, Pennsylvania, during the winter of 1777–78. Despite the recent American victory at Saratoga, morale was extremely low.

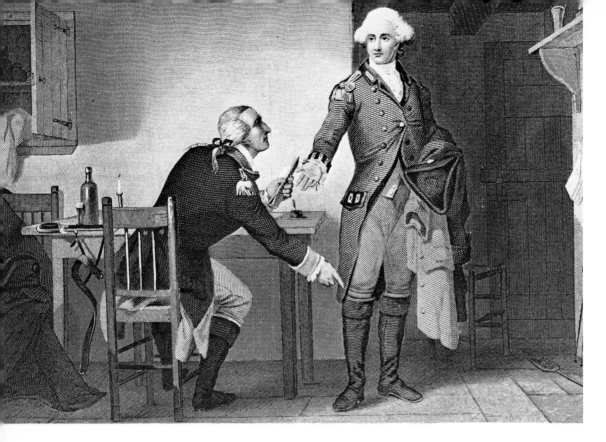

The hero of Saratoga, Benedict Arnold (seated), persuades Major John Andre of the British army to hide incriminating documents in his boot. Arnold conspired with Andre to hand over to the British the American fort at West Point, but the plot was discovered and both men were captured. Arnold escaped and went on to fight with the British; Andre was hanged as a spy.

The war over, Hamilton returned to Albany and set himself to preparing for a career. He decided on law. After obtaining a dispensation from the provision that required prospective attorneys to serve an apprenticeship of three years, Hamilton mastered the volumes of material necessary to pass his bar examination in three months and was admitted to the bar in July 1782. In the process he prepared a study guide, entitled *Practical Proceedings in the Supreme Court of the State of New York*, which was so comprehensive that it was subsequently used as a manual by attorneys.

Hamilton's war record, family connections and careful nurturing of powerful friends (such as Robert Morris and John Jay), and his own temperament and inclination combined to ensure that he was never out of public life for long. Morris, who had signed the Declaration of Independence, played a crucial role in financing the revolutionary war, and was currently the nation's superintendent of finance, secured Hamilton an appointment as the Continental Congress's tax collector in New York.

The pay was meager and the task — to convince the state government to actually dole out the money it had appropriated for the operation of the Confederation government — next to impossible. Hamilton resigned in frustration after four months, confirmed in his belief that a much stronger national government needed to be created.

At about this time the New York legislature chose Hamilton as one of its five delegates to the Continental Congress, then meeting in Philadelphia, where he served from late November 1782 until the following July. What Hamilton saw in Congress did not inspire confidence in the future of the nation. Few of the delegates bothered to attend the daily sessions — two of the New York representatives never even arrived in Philadelphia — and many of those present were demoralized by Congress's powerlessness to remedy the nation's dire financial condition, which had been worsened by Britain's closing of its West Indies ports to American shipping and a proliferation of worthless paper money and bonds. Hamilton did discover some congressmen who were seriously pondering solutions, most notably James Madison of Virginia. His own beliefs on the need for an authentic national government had not changed and were delineated in six essays, known collectively as *The Continentalist*, written shortly before his term in Congress. Hamilton again advocated the creation of a federal system, with powers to be shared by the states and the national government.

At the Battle of Yorktown in October 1781 Hamilton led a bayonet charge that captured a British artillery redoubt. The American victory at Yorktown marked the triumphant conclusion of the colonists' War of Independence, although it took two years to negotiate a peace treaty.

Philadelphia shipping merchant Robert Morris served as superintendent of finance under the Articles of Confederation. Like Hamilton, he regarded the restoration of public credit as essential to establishing a strong national government. Morris was influential in securing Hamilton an appointment as receiver of continental taxes for New York.

To those who warned of the danger of concentrating too much governmental power at the national level, Hamilton replied that although "too much power leads to despotism . . . too little leads to anarchy, and both eventually to the ruin of the people." Hamilton believed that at the very minimum the national government must possess the right to regulate interstate trade, appoint its own officials, govern America's vast western territories, impose tariffs, and levy and collect its own taxes. Under the Articles of Confederation, Congress was empowered to do none of this. In the conclusion of *The Continentalist*, Hamilton called on the states to assemble a national convention to rework the Articles.

Congress's powerlessness was demonstrated in March of 1783. Although combat had ceased with the victory at Yorktown, no peace treaty had been signed, and with British troops still present in New York City and several of the states, the Continental Army had remained intact. On the 12th of that month word reached Philadelphia that agreement on a peace treaty with Great Britain was imminent. Angered by the fact that a bankrupt Congress was unable to give them the back pay and bonuses they had been promised, the soldiers of the Continental Army had refused to disband. The prospect of a formal peace brought the crisis to a head. Many of the soldiers had gone deeply in debt during the time they served and faced bankruptcy or prison if they were forced to return home without the money they were owed. Hoping to use the prospect of a mutinous army to spur the state governments into approving the type of financial reorganization Hamilton had been advocating, certain congressmen encouraged the army in its unrest.

Hamilton was among those who considered using the army as an instrument to force the state governments to either provide funds or allow Congress to impose taxes that would enable it to begin payment to the nation's creditors — including the war veterans — but he eventually rejected the idea. Although he continued to press for financial reforms, Hamilton feared the chaos a rebellious army might unleash. When a meeting was announced for March

15 at which the army was to decide on its future course of action, Hamilton encouraged Washington to be there "to bring order, perhaps even good, out of confusion." While sympathetic to his soldiers' grievances, Washington believed Congress should be given time to make good on its promises.

The March 15 meeting took place at army head-quarters at Newburgh, New York. Washington attended and begged his men not to take rash action or "any measure which viewed in the calm light of reason, will lessen the dignity and sully the glory you have hitherto maintained." Any further thought of revolt ended when the beloved Washington, having difficulty reading his speech, reached into his pocket for a pair of spectacles and said, "Gentlemen, you must pardon me. I have grown gray in your service and now find myself growing blind." The successful negotiations with Britain also helped defuse the situation, as they removed the army's chief trump card; namely, the refusal to fight should hostilities resume. The army received some back pay in the form of notes personally guaranteed by Robert Morris, and most of the soldiers simply went home. In June a group of disgruntled veterans marched on Philadelphia and besieged Congress, demanding back wages. When the state government of Pennsylvania, offended by Hamilton's suggestion that it bore the principal responsibility for the crisis, ignored his demands that it call in the state militia to disperse the soldiers, Congress was forced to flee to Princeton. As Congress was nearing the end of its term, many of its members went home.

His term over, Hamilton returned to the Schuyler mansion in Albany, but he was not to stay long. He soon moved his family — there was now a young son, Philip — to a house at 57 Wall Street in New York City. The new home also served as Hamilton's office for his law practice, which thrived, because of both Hamilton's supreme abilities and his influential connections. Chancellor of New York James Kent, in 1832, recalling the many lawyers he had seen practice, named Hamilton the best, citing "his profound penetration, his power of analysis" and "the comprehensive grasp and strength of his under-

James Madison of Virginia met Hamilton at the Continental Congress of 1782. The two were initially great allies, agreeing on the need to revamp the Articles of Confederation and then leading the fight for ratification of the Constitution.

standing." A prominent judge of the day, Ambrose Spencer, felt that Hamilton's creativity and reasoning power made him the equal of the distinguished American statesman Daniel Webster, who before his political career was widely regarded as the nation's most able trial attorney.

Within a few months of opening his office Hamilton had many of the richest merchants and landowners in New York and New Jersey for clients, including John Jay, Robert Morris, and his wealthy brother-in-law John Church. His caseload included wills, property closings, and criminal proceedings as well as more than 60 cases involving former Tories. One of these, *Rutgers v. Waddington*, still holds an important place in American constitutional law.

After independence, the New York State legislature passed a series of laws that authorized the confiscation of Loyalists' property, erased debts owed Loyalists, and allowed those who had fled New York City during the British occupation to sue for damages Loyalists who had made use of their property. Although arguing the rights of Tories was extremely unpopular and politically unwise, Hamilton believed the legislation to be contrary to all established principles of law. He also felt that the legislation hurt the new nation's economy, as thousands of formerly Loyalist merchants, many of whom were quite wealthy, fled the country rather than face confiscation of their property.

Washington's headquarters near Newburgh, New York, where the Continental Army encamped following the revolutionary war. Angered by Congress's failure to provide back pay and bonuses, the army threatened to mutiny in the spring of 1783, but Washington intervened to ward off the uprising.

Hamilton's political connections contributed to the success of his law practice, but his greatest assets were his immense abilities of deductive reasoning and analysis, a comprehensive understanding of legal principles, and the power of persuasive oratory.

The defendant in *Rutgers v. Waddington*, Joshua Waddington, had been licensed by the British army to run a brewery it had seized from the plaintiff, Elizabeth Rutgers, during its occupation of New York City. Rutgers was suing for the equivalent of the rental value of her property for the time — seven years — it had been in the army and Waddington's control. When the case was heard on August 7, 1784, Hamilton presented a twofold argument. He urged the suit be dismissed on the grounds that the actions of Waddington and the British army did not violate customary practice under international law. His more important contention was that as the New York legislation under which the suit had been brought violated the terms of the peace treaty the Continental Congress had concluded with Great Britain, the legislation was null and void and the plaintiff had no standing to bring suit. Hamilton's argument had important ramifications regarding the concept of state sovereignty, as it implied that in this case as well as others the interests of the national government in performing its legitimate functions could outweigh those of the states. Although the judge awarded Rutgers partial damages, stating that the judiciary had no power to overturn an act of the legislature, Hamilton's argument would ultimately be accepted as a fundamental principle of American constitutional law.

THE

FEDERALIST;

A COLLECTION

OF *S. Chase*

ESSAYS,

WRITTEN IN FAVOUR OF THE

NEW CONSTITUTION,

AS AGREED UPON BY THE FEDERAL CONVENTION,
SEPTEMBER 17, 1787.

IN TWO VOLUMES.

VOL. I.

NEW-YORK:

PRINTED AND SOLD BY J. AND A. McLEAN,
No. 41, HANOVER-SQUARE.
M,DCC,LXXXVIII.

3

The Constitution

Despite his willingness to defend unpopular causes, by the mid-1780s Hamilton had become one of the most prominent men in New York. In partnership with John Church, he helped found the Bank of New York in 1784. His position on state sovereignty notwithstanding, he was selected to the state legislature as an assemblyman from New York City in 1786. He continued to press his argument for reform of the Articles of Confederation, which he termed a "system . . . radically vicious and unsound." When Virginia — largely at the behest of James Madison — suggested that representatives from the states meet at Annapolis, Maryland, in September 1786 "for the purpose of forming such regulations of trade as may be judged necessary to promote the general interest," Hamilton eagerly accepted the chance to represent New York.

Only 12 delegates from 5 states bothered to make the journey to Annapolis. Because so few states were represented, it was quickly agreed that the meeting had to be postponed. Seeing opportunity in the convention's failure, Hamilton and Madison took the

The frail and tottering edifice [of the Confederation] seems ready to fall upon our heads and to crush us beneath its ruins.
—ALEXANDER HAMILTON

A first edition of *The Federalist*, the collection of essays written by Hamilton, James Madison, and John Jay — under the collective pseudonym Publius — to convince New Yorkers to ratify the Constitution. Thomas Jefferson called it the best commentary "on the principles of government which ever was written."

lead in dramatizing the critical situation confronting the nation, which went beyond the need for regulation of interstate and international trade. They emphasized to the other delegates the need for a meeting to consider reform of the Articles. Before the conference adjourned, the delegates adopted a report written by Hamilton proposing that a recommendation be made to Congress to call for all 13 states to send representatives to a convention "to devise such further provisions as shall appear . . . necessary to render the constitution of the federal government adequate to the exigencies of the Union."

Seeing in the call for a constitutional convention the likelihood of its own demise, the Continental Congress was in no hurry to act on Hamilton's proposal. While Congress dallied, farmers in western Massachusetts, most of whom were former soldiers heavily in debt, took up arms against the state government. Led by Daniel Shays, a revolutionary war veteran, the rebels prevented courts from sitting and thus rendering further judgments against farmers for indebtedness. The governor was finally forced to call out troops to quell the uprising. The national government's impotence in the face of Shays' Rebellion — lacking money or an army, Congress had been unable to respond to Massachusetts's appeals for help — frightened many of the state governments into support for the constitutional convention. The rebellion also helped move the nation's merchants, businessmen, and creditors toward active support for the proposed meeting. Several states had issued essentially worthless paper money and authorized its use for the payment of debts. Fearing that popular unrest of the Massachusetts type would encourage further disrespect for property rights, the monied classes joined in the call for a constitutional convention. On February 21, 1787, Congress invited the states to send delegates to Philadelphia in May "for the sole and express purpose of revising the Articles of Confederation." All but Rhode Island complied. Hamilton, because of his father-in-law's power in the New York Senate, was chosen to be one of New York's three delegates.

> *We shall blend the advantages of a monarchy and a republic in our constitution.*
> —ALEXANDER HAMILTON

Hamilton sat quietly and observed the proceedings of the Constitutional Convention for almost a month before speaking. Most of the discussion focused on the structure of the new government: Should the legislature have one or two branches? Should each state have equal representation in the national legislature or should representation be proportional, based on population? Would the legislature be popularly elected? How long would the national executive serve? How extensive would the powers of the national judiciary be? As far as Hamilton was concerned, these matters skirted rather than addressed the real issue: How much more powerful than the states should the new national government be? Unable to restrain his impatience any longer, on June 18 Hamilton delivered a five-hour speech designed to answer his own question. In designing a national government, he told his fellow

Hamilton (center) reads the constitution he wrote for the Bank of New York, which he helped found in 1784, to the bank's officers. Seated (left to right) they are: William Maxwell, Thomas Stoughton, Major General Alexander McDougall, Samuel Franklin, Comfort Sands, and William Seton.

41

Shays' Rebellion was an uprising of western Massachusetts farmers angered by economic policies that benefited merchants and increased their own indebtedness. The rebels attacked local courts, the state supreme court, and the state arsenal before being routed. Here a government supporter tussles with a rebel.

delegates, "we ought to go as far in order to attain stability and permanency, as republican principles will admit." The new national government should be so "completely sovereign" that it would "annihilate the state distinctions and state operations."

Hamilton's emphasis was on permanency and stability, and he expressed mistrust for popular sovereignty. "Men love power," he said. "Give all the power to the many, they will repress the few. Give all the power to the few, they will repress the many. The voice of the people has been said to be the voice of God, but it is not true in fact. The people are turbulent and ever changing; they seldom judge or determine right."

Why debate what the structure of a new central government should be when a perfect model already existed? As, Hamilton stated, "the British government [was] the best in the world," the new system should strive to emulate it. Hamilton proposed a bicameral legislature, in which members of the upper house would be elected for life by electors chosen by property holders. Members of the lower house would be elected for three years, with all males eligible to vote. His most controversial proposal regarded the national executive. Under Hamilton's plan the executive would be chosen by electors — who in turn would be chosen by the voters — and would serve for life. He would possess the power to veto all acts of the legislature and would appoint all state governors, who also would serve for life. To many this sounded close to monarchy, still a dirty word in a nation proud of its victory over the tyranny of King George III of Britain and wary of the dangers of investing too much power in the central government. Hamilton argued that the executive had to possess considerable power if the government was to be as strong as it needed to be and that there was no surer way to insure that a chief executive would not abuse his office than to make the position so attractive he would "risk too much to acquire more [power]."

Considering the popular opinion of the time, it was probably fortunate for Hamilton that the convention's proceedings were secret — even so, he would spend much of his life refuting charges that he was an elitist and monarchist infatuated with the political and economic system of Great Britain — but his fellow delegates were not shocked by his proposals. Similar opinions had already been expressed by other representatives, and Hamilton's proposed government — which allowed for both the expression of the popular will and the exercise of strong leadership — reflected much of the conventional political wisdom of the day. For example, Elbridge Gerry of Massachusetts had stated that "the evils we [the country] experience flow from the excesses of democracy." The lawyer and financier Gouverneur Morris called Hamilton's speech "the most able and impressive he had ever heard." William Samuel Johnson, a representative from Connecticut, said Hamilton "had been praised by everybody [and] supported by none," but Hamilton's influence had been greater than Johnson supposed. As he had intended, Hamilton had focused the debate on the question of the strength, rather than the form, of the national government, and the Constitutional Convention would ultimately bestow the new government with more power than hitherto contemplated.

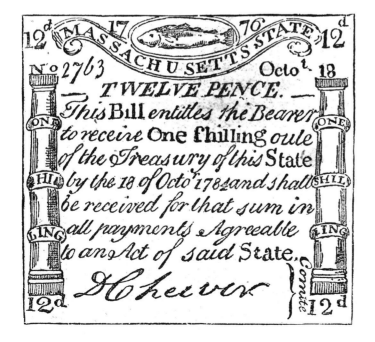

Paper money issued by the state of Massachusetts during the revolutionary war. Such currency was unsecured by gold or silver reserves and was essentially worthless. Several states continued to print money after the war; the resulting financial confusion led Hamilton and others to call for a strong central government that could overhaul the nation's economy.

George Clinton served as New York's governor from 1777 to 1795 and again from 1801 to 1804 before becoming vice-president under Thomas Jefferson and James Madison. In 1787–88 Clinton led the New York opposition to the Constitution's ratification.

As the other two members of the New York contingent had been handpicked by Governor George Clinton, an unyielding advocate of state sovereignty, Hamilton's views put him in the minority among his own delegation. With each state delegation having only one vote, Hamilton had little opportunity to influence the proceedings any further. He returned home at the end of June to take care of legal business. Despite his disapproval of the specific proposals being considered by the convention, Hamilton remained a supporter of its goals. When Clinton published attacks on the Constitutional Convention in New York City newspapers, Hamilton defended the convention's aims and the work of the delegates in a series of articles written under the pen names "A Republican" and "Caesar."

Hamilton returned to Philadelphia in early September, in time for the convention's final deliberations. The dispute between advocates of the so-called Virginia plan, who called for scrapping the Articles in favor of a new constitution providing for a national executive, national judiciary, and, most important, a bicameral legislature in which representation would be based proportionally on the population of the individual states; and advocates of the New Jersey plan, who called for reform of the Articles and a unicameral legislature in which each state would have equal representation, had been settled by the Connecticut Compromise. By the terms of the compromise the legislature took essentially its present form — two houses, with equal representation in the Senate and proportional representation in the House of Representatives. Both the states and the people were represented in the legislature. The people directly elected delegates to the House, while the individual legislatures elected their state's two senators. (Direct, popular election of senators was not adopted until the ratification of the Seventeenth Amendment, in 1913.) Hamilton took part in the major debate of the convention's final days, over the method of election of the president. He spoke in favor of having a body of electors, rather than Congress, select the president, although his plan differed somewhat from the plan adopted by the convention. Under the Constitution the electoral college was to be chosen by the individual state legislatures, with each state receiving as many electors as it had representatives in Congress. (Today the electors are chosen by popular vote.) The final document created a powerful national executive branch while at the same time providing the legislature — which embodied the interests of the people and the states — with enough power to check the executive should he overstep his bounds.

Hamilton spent his last days in Philadelphia ironing out minor compromises that he hoped would enable the Constitution to receive the convention's unanimous support. He and the other delegates were aware that it would be difficult to obtain the approval of the nine state legislatures needed for ratification. The opposition of such important delegates as Virginia's Edmund Randolph and George Mason and Massachusett's Elbridge Gerry to the final draft of the Constitution, coupled with the refusal of such prominent Americans as Patrick

The fiery revolutionary orator Patrick Henry was one of several prominent Americans who opposed the new Constitution. He is shown here making his 1765 speech denouncing British tyranny. "If this be treason," he retorted to listeners who branded his speech as such, "make the most of it."

The Ninth *PILLAR* erected !

" The Ratification of the Conventions of nine States, fhall be fufficient for the eftablifh-ment of this Conftitution, between the States fo ratifying the fame." *Art.* vii.

INCIPIENT MAGNI PROCEDERE MENSES.

If it is not up it will rife.

The Attraction muft be irrefiftible

DEL. PEN. N.JER. GEOR. CON. MASSA. MARY. S.ºCARO. N.HAMP. VIRG. N. YORK

This 1788 cartoon celebrates the ratification of the Constitution with the approval of New Hampshire, "the ninth pillar," while recognizing the importance of Virginia and New York to the ultimate success of the Union.

Henry, Samuel Adams, and Richard Henry Lee to even attend the convention, made ratification even more unlikely.

Hamilton did not approve of many of the Constitution's features, but he considered it a vast improvement on the Articles of Confederation and believed its ratification essential to the nation's well-being. He found the opposition of others at this stage difficult to fathom. Speaking of his own misgivings, he said, "No man's ideas were more remote from the plan than [my] own were known to be," but urged support by asking, "Is it possible to deliberate between anarchy and Convulsion on one side, and the chance of good to be expected of the plan on the other?" Unswayed, the three prominent opponents refused to sign the final document. Writing some 44 years later, James Madison, who more than any other man was responsible for the Constitution, remarked on Hamilton's selflessness and willingness to compromise to secure a document he believed would benefit his nation: "If his theory of government deviated from the republican standard, he had the candour to avow it, and the greater merit of co-operating faithfully and maturing in supporting a system that was not his choice."

Lively and spirited public debate on the wisdom of ratification began almost immediately. Newspapers made space for the full text of the Constitution, which was often read aloud and debated, section by section, in village squares and taverns. Hamilton decided that a public defense of the proposed new government was needed in order "to cultivate a favorable disposition in the citizens at large" and recruited James Madison and John Jay to help him write essays in support of the Constitution. The first appeared in New York City's *Independent Journal* on October 27, 1787, and new pieces were published several times a week until April 1788. All 85 of the essays, which were collected and published for the first time in 1788 as *The Federalist*, appeared under the pen name "Publius." Legend has it that Hamilton wrote the first essay in the cabin of his sloop while returning from Albany. John Jay wrote the next four essays but was able to contribute only

The *Hamilton*, named after the Constitution's foremost champion, passes beneath members of Congress atop the fort at Bowling Green during New York City's ratification parade, July 1788.

> *The security of the public liberty must consist in such a distribution of the sovereign power as will make it morally impossible for one part to gain ascendancy over the others, or for the whole to unite in a scheme of usurpation.*
> —ALEXANDER HAMILTON

one more due to illness. That left the bulk of the work to Hamilton and Madison. Although authorship of certain of the *Federalist* essays is still in question, it is likely that Hamilton wrote 51 of the articles, Madison, 29. Intended to convince a wary public that the system of checks and balances embodied in the new Constitution would correct the defects of the Articles of Confederation and guarantee the nation's "political prosperity" while preserving the essential sovereignty of the states and protecting individual rights, *The Federalist* has endured as the most authoritative explanation of the American political system.

The convention decreed that each state was to hold an election for delegates who would decide on the question of ratification. Soon after the first *Federalist* article appeared, Delaware became the first state to ratify. Pennsylvania and New Jersey followed suit before the end of 1787, and they were soon joined by five others. Ratification was achieved when New Hampshire voted in favor of the new government on June 17, 1788, but the remaining four states were free to choose not to join the proposed union, and successful implementation of the new government was unlikely without the support of the wealthy and populous states of Virginia and New York. Following long debate, James Madison secured Virginia's vote to ratify on June 25, 1788, after promising that Congress would take up Virginia's demand that explicit safeguards of individual liberties (known afterward as the Bill of Rights) be included in the Constitution.

That left New York as the last large undecided state. Its importance as a trade center and strategic location between New England and the southern states made it indispensable to the success of the proposed new nation. With the exception of New York City and the surrounding areas, the state was solidly anti-Constitution. In the election for the ratification convention — the first conducted in New York on the basis of universal manhood suffrage — New Yorkers voted 16,000 to 7,000 against ratification, electing 46 anti-Federalist delegates to only 19 supporters of the Constitution. As the Constitution's most prolific defender, Hamilton was the natural leader of New York's Federalists (the name adopted by the Constitution's advocates).

The ratification convention met in Poughkeepsie in June and July of 1788. As at the other state ratification assemblies, debate was animated and sometimes bitter. The challenge of fighting against seemingly insurmountable odds brought out the best in Hamilton, who was aided by John Jay and New York's chancellor, Robert Livingston. George Clinton directed the opposition forces. Day after day, in speech after speech, Hamilton defended the Constitution and demolished the logic of its opponents, who attacked the document as a threat to individual and state liberty and denigrated its supporters as aristocrats. In addition to Hamilton's brilliance, the Federalists had momentum working for them. News that Virginia had ratified reached New York on July 2. Rumors that the downstate region would secede and apply to the Union for membership as a separate state if New York failed to ratify moved even more delegates into the Federalist camp. After receiving a promise from Madison that the Bill of Rights amendments would receive Congress's "early and mature consideration," the New York convention voted on July 26, by a slim 30-27 vote, to ratify the Constitution.

As the country celebrated the birth of its new government with mammoth parades and parties, the Constitution's supporters praised Hamilton for his magnificent performance in New York. There had been little doubt among Federalists in New York City that their cause would triumph. Plans for a celebratory parade had been under way since shortly after the convention's opening, and the actual event took place three days before ratification was secured. The centerpiece of the parade was a replica of a ship, drawn by 10 horses and manned by 30 sailors. It was called the *Hamilton* in honor of the Constitution's champion. Still busy in Poughkeepsie, Hamilton did not attend, but his former sponsor Nicholas Cruger was among the spectators who watched proudly as the young republic feted its newest hero.

> *Power controuled or abridged is almost always the rival and enemy of that power by which it is controuled and abridged.*
> —ALEXANDER HAMILTON

4

Finance Minister

Attendance at the New York convention in Pough-keepsie kept Hamilton from New York City for six weeks. With the ratification battle won, Hamilton relaxed, attended to his law practice and growing family, and waited to be offered an important post in the new government. Although George Washington was expected to be the virtually unanimous choice to become the nation's first president, he had announced his retirement from public life in 1783 and now expressed reluctance about accepting the presidency should it be offered. In correspondence with his former commanding officer, Hamilton cited Washington's duty to support the new Constitution as reason for him to accept this new challenge: "On your acceptance of the office of the President the success of the new government in its material commencement may materially depend." Washington in turn assured Hamilton that he intended to rely on his expertise and advice in carrying out his new duties.

Washington took the oath of office in New York City, the nation's temporary capital, on April 30, 1789. There was, of course, no protocol yet established for the office of the president, and Washington asked Hamilton how he felt a president should behave while performing various public ceremonies.

Seldom has any minister excited in a higher or more extensive degree than Colonel Hamilton the opposite passions of love and hate.
—JOHN MARSHALL
historian

Spectators cheer George Washington as he steps onto the balcony of Federal Hall, in lower Manhattan, on his inauguration day, April 30, 1789. That Washington should head the new government was one of the few aspects of its formation the entire nation was in agreement on.

Washington (with right hand on Bible) takes the oath of office from New York State chancellor Robert Livingston (front left) while Vice-president John Adams (front right) looks on. The new nation had no precedent for such ceremonies; Washington turned to Hamilton for advice on what protocol should be observed.

Hamilton replied with candor and tact, advising strict adherence to the rules of etiquette and protocol as practiced in Europe. Fully expecting an appointment in Washington's government, Hamilton spent the summer of 1789 waiting for Congress to establish the various government departments and putting his business affairs in order. Hamilton asked Robert Troup, a King's College classmate and close friend, to prepare himself to manage the affairs of his legal practice.

A little more than a week after Congress established the Treasury Department, Washington asked Hamilton to be its head. The position was precisely the one Hamilton had wanted. Not only was his the largest government department, but he had been given broad latitude by Congress in directing its operations and he believed that "most of the important measures of every Government are connected with the Treasury." Certain that during Washington's first term the great issues confronting the nation would revolve around questions of finance, Hamilton reasoned that whoever occupied the office of secretary of the Treasury would be in a position to determine the focus of national debate.

To Hamilton's mind, the combined foreign, national, and state debt was the greatest problem Washington's government faced. Congress agreed. The act that established the Treasury Department required its head to report "in person or in writing" on any subject referred to him by the House or Senate and to submit periodic proposals on the fiscal operations of his department. On September 21, 1789, just 10 days after Hamilton's appointment, the House of Representatives, noting that "an adequate provision for the public credit" was a "matter of high importance to the national honor and prosperity," ordered Hamilton to "prepare a plan for that purpose."

Three and a half months later Hamilton submitted the 40,000-word *Report Relative to a Provision for the Support of Public Credit* to Congress. Most congressmen had expected some modest proposals for handling the public debt. Instead, Hamilton had developed a detailed blueprint for solving the nation's fiscal problems. Few congressmen could argue with Hamilton's overall intent — to restore the nation's financial credibility by paying off its creditors. "States, like individuals, who observe their engagements are respected and trusted," Hamilton said. Still, the specifics of his plan aroused controversy and occupied Congress for the rest of its term.

The United States owed approximately $11 million abroad, the majority to the French royal treasury and Dutch bankers. The several debtor states — Massachusetts, South Carolina, and Connecticut had the largest outstanding obligations — owed some $25 million from the revolutionary war. Finally, Congress owed more than $40 million in domestic debt, in the form of worthless paper money, bonds, and promissory notes issued during the war.

There was virtually unanimous agreement that the foreign debt had to be paid off in full in order to establish the credit of the United States abroad, but there was considerable opposition to paying back American holders of the nation's domestic debt. The bonds Congress had issued during the war — called loan office certificates — promised to pay

He perceived, as his critics did not, the connection between national income and the national debt and he recognized that there was no more certain way of disposing of the debt than by stimulating the productive forces of the country.
—JOHN C. MILLER
historian

Washington (far right) confers with his first cabinet. Its members were (left to right) Secretary of War Henry Knox, Secretary of State Thomas Jefferson, Attorney General Edmund Randolph, and Hamilton, the secretary of the Treasury.

the holder at some point in the future the amount printed on the face of the paper plus interest at a certain rate. These bonds had been sold to raise money for the government or given to men to induce them to enlist. During the war and the depression that followed, many of the original bondholders had been forced to sell their bonds for whatever they could get. Speculators — most of them northeastern stockbrokers, bankers, and businessmen — willing to gamble on their future possible worth bought up the bonds for as little as 15 or 20 cents on the dollar. This meant that if Hamilton's plan for paying the bonds off at full face value plus interest was adopted, speculators, not the farmers, small merchants, and soldiers who had originally been given the bonds, would reap huge profits. Not surprisingly, opponents of Hamilton's plan argued that it favored moneyed interests at the expense of farmers and the Northeast at the expense of the rest of the nation.

Madison suggested paying bondholders differing amounts based upon when they had bought their securities, but Congress rejected his idea because there was no way to be sure when someone had come into possession of a bond. Ultimately, Hamilton's approach was accepted.

Hamilton's proposal that the federal government assume the remaining war debts of the states drew similar fire. States such as Virginia and Maryland, who had paid off their debts, were infuriated. Although Hamilton replied that because the war had been fought for the benefit of all the states, the government that now represented those states should pay off their war debts, Congress was soon deadlocked over the issue, with Madison, representing Virginia, again leading the opposition. Aware that if too much time was lost his program would be defeated, Hamilton took the initiative.

On June 20 Hamilton met with Madison at a dinner party at Thomas Jefferson's New York City home. The other great issue occupying Congress at the time was the permanent location of the capital. New York City, Philadelphia, and a new location along the Potomac River were the competing sites.

Hamilton's interests and abilities made him perfectly suited for the position of secretary of the Treasury, which he regarded as the most important cabinet post. During Washington's second term he was also acting secretary of war and assumed many of the duties of the secretary of state.

Hamilton (standing at right) outlines his plans for financial reform to Washington (far left) and the rest of the cabinet. Jefferson (center) opposed Hamilton's proposals on the grounds that they depended upon the federal government exercising powers that the Constitution did not explicitly grant.

Madison and Jefferson, who were close political allies, both favored the Potomac site. In exchange for the Virginians' support on the assumption of state debts, Hamilton promised Madison and Jefferson to secure votes in Congress in favor of locating the capital on the Potomac. They agreed, asking only for slight modifications in Hamilton's program that would financially benefit Virginia. Four separate acts made Hamilton's program law in July 1790.

Funding the total debt meant exchanging old bonds for new ones. The new bonds went mainly to the same group — bankers and wealthy merchants — who had profited from trade in the old paper, giving rise to renewed criticism of Hamilton's economic policies. The charges were the same — that Hamilton had intentionally concentrated wealth in the hands of the nation's merchants and businessmen. Hamilton dismissed the charges. He believed that given human nature and differences in talent and opportunity, inequalities in the distribution of wealth would always exist. Hamilton believed that human beings were motivated primarily by self-interest, a view that was shared by Madison and permeates their *Federalist* essays. (Interestingly enough, Madison's motivation for locating the capital on the Potomac was in good part due to his having purchased large tracts of land near the future site.) The trick was somehow to harness that self-interest to the common good, which Hamilton believed his economic program had done. By paying off the wartime bonds, Hamilton assured the new government of the business class's support and in the process channeled the self-interest of the business class in realizing profits into achieving the greater goal of reestablishing the nation's credit. The business class already controlled much of the nation's productive capital, but now its economic prosperity was tied to that of the federal government and the nation as a whole. With credit reestablished and the nation on a sound financial footing, the United States was free to realize its enormous productive capacity, which Hamilton believed would ultimately guarantee greater prosperity for all of its citizens.

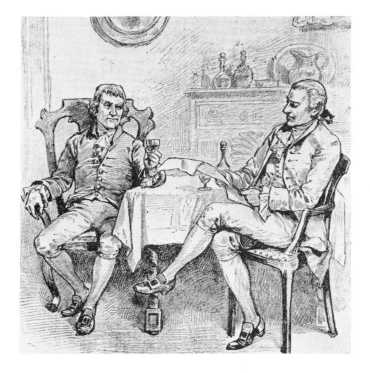

Jefferson (left) and Madison (right) discuss the future site of the nation's capital. The two Virginians wanted a new capital city to be built on the Potomac River. Hamilton agreed to their proposal in exchange for their support of federal assumption of state war debts, and Congress voted to move the capital from Philadelphia to what is now Washington, D.C.

This Philadelphia building housed the first U.S. mint. The Constitution reserved the right to coin money to the federal government. Although it was Hamilton who devised a comprehensive plan for the creation and circulation of a national currency, the mint initially was placed under the jurisdiction of Jefferson's State Department.

Hamilton revealed the next phase of his economic plan in December 1790. He proposed to Congress that the United States create a national bank modeled after the Bank of England. The federal government would put in $2 million of the bank's $10 million capital and appoint one-fifth of the bank's directors. Private investors would supply the rest of the capital and elect the other directors. In return for the use of the government's money, the bank would serve as the government's financial agent, providing a safe place to deposit the government's cash and lending the government money to cover operating expenses between tax revenue receipts. The bank's notes would serve as legal tender and supplement the dwindling supply of *specie* (gold and silver coin).

The creation of the national bank aroused opposition in Congress, as Hamilton's critics again charged that his proposal would primarily benefit businessmen and speculators, and especially the Northeast. Hamilton believed the national bank would strengthen the federal government and the national economy. He thought that he was acting in the interests of the nation as a whole, but his unwillingness to consider the problems of the nation's agrarian sector and his indifference to class, state, and regional interests were making implacable enemies of people who had once been his allies.

At the Constitutional Convention Edmund Randolph was the chief proponent of the Virginia Plan. He refused to sign the Constitution, although he later supported its ratification. Under Washington he served as attorney general and then as secretary of state after Jefferson's resignation.

Washington confers with Hamilton and Robert Morris at his New York City home. The president's confidence in his Treasury secretary only increased Jefferson's opposition to Hamilton's policies.

The most significant argument against the national bank rested on constitutional rather than economic grounds. Madison argued that the establishment of a national bank was unconstitutional because such an institution was not mentioned in the Constitution. Because powers not granted to the national government were reserved to the states, only the states had the power to charter banks. Congress did not agree. By mid-February of 1791 both the Senate and the House had given their approval.

Washington had been made uneasy by the constitutionality issue, however, and decided to seek the counsel of Jefferson, then secretary of state, and

Attorney General Edmund Randolph before signing the bill into law. Both men pronounced the idea unconstitutional. The assumption of state debts may have been necessary, said Jefferson, but the establishment of a national bank was going too far. Because the Constitution did not specifically give Congress the power to establish a bank, it should not be allowed.

Before making a final decision on the matter, Washington decided to give Hamilton an opportunity to rebut Jefferson's strict interpretation. After a week of intense work, Hamilton submitted his answer to the president. As might be expected, Hamilton focused not on the limits of the government's power but on the extent of its sovereignty. He argued that inherent in the very definition of the new national government was the right to do everything necessary and proper to carry out any of the powers granted it in the Constitution. The bank, he reasoned, was a necessary and proper way to borrow money and to regulate the currency, both of which were powers the Constitution had plainly assigned to Congress. Hamilton concluded his critique with the observation that Jefferson's constitutional literalness would destroy "the just and indispensable authority of the United States." His viewpoint subsequently became known as the *broad* or *loose constructionist* interpretation of the Constitution. Hamilton's relentless, point-by-point demolition of Jefferson's argument convinced Washington, who signed the national bank into law on February 25.

It was a glorious time for Hamilton. His economic policies had been adopted, and he had succeeded in becoming the president's closest and most trusted adviser, referred to by some as "the prime minister." A college was named after him in upstate New York, and Dartmouth and Harvard colleges conferred law degrees upon him. Yet Hamilton's genius was not for politics. His confidence — some called it arrogance — outraged his opponents, and his certainty that he, and sometimes he alone, was acting with the nation's interests in mind blinded him to the enmity that was developing toward him.

> *Public utility is more truly the object of public banks than private profit.*
> —ALEXANDER HAMILTON

5

Clashing Ambitions

The final piece of Hamilton's three-pronged plan for the long-range economic development of America was contained in his *Report on Manufactures*, which he submitted to Congress in December 1791. Almost a year earlier, in January 1790, the House of Representatives had directed him to "prepare a proper plan . . . for the encouragement and promotion of such manufactories as will tend to render the United States independent of other nations for essential, particularly military, supplies." For the third and last time, Hamilton enlarged the scope of Congress's order to fit his own agenda. He submitted a comprehensive survey of American industry along with a summary of the advantages and disadvantages of the government's encouragement of certain types of industrial development. The message of the *Report on Manufactures* was clear: Industrial development in America was necessary in order to secure a balanced, strong, and self-reliant national economy, and the government should institute a protective tariff (tax on imports) to promote that end.

> The Report on Manufactures was the last of Hamilton's great triad of reports and to many students his finest performance.
> —JACOB E. COOKE
> Hamilton biographer

Hamilton's interpretation of the Constitution rested on his belief that the most important power it granted the federal government was the right to act. Jefferson was equally convinced that "that government is best which governs least." The clash between these two viewpoints gave birth to the first American political parties.

Federal Hall in New York City served briefly as the nation's capital. The government moved to Philadelphia in 1790, before settling permanently in Washington, D.C., in 1800.

Hamilton fully expected Congress to support his vision of an industrialized America by voting for the tariff. After all, his first two proposals had been approved, and their implementation had proved his judgment correct. The American economy was booming. Now that capital and credit were provided for, all Congress had to do was pass a tariff high enough to keep out cheap European manufactured goods. Protection from foreign competition would encourage investment in factories and manufacturing enterprises in this country. The resulting growth in America's productive capacity would lead to economic self-reliance and increased national prosperity.

Hamilton was ahead of his time. While his vision was trained on Europe's burgeoning Industrial Revolution and its implications for the future of the United States, many Americans had a different view of their nation, one rooted in the country's predominantly agrarian past. Thomas Jefferson was the most eloquent and prominent supporter of such a position. He believed, as he wrote in his *Notes on the State of Virginia*, that "those who labour in the earth are the chosen people of God." For Jefferson, those who worked the soil were free from the vicissitudes of public demand and the subservience that wage labor engendered. They were also at liberty to cultivate the civic virtues embodied by the many planter-statesmen from his home state who had risen to positions of leadership in the new nation — himself, George Washington, James Madison, Edmund Randolph, Richard Henry Lee, and Patrick Henry, just to name a few — and were distanced from the corrupting influence of the cities. Of course, Jefferson's "natural aristocracy" consisted of only a very few men, and the leisure time available for public service and the development of the "higher virtues" was afforded them by the use of slave labor. Philosophical considerations aside, planters and farmers opposed Hamilton's tariff because its implementation would have meant higher prices for manufactured goods. Hamilton also discovered that northern merchants were not unanimous in their support for the tariff. Those who made their living in foreign trade sided with the farmers and planters. Congress voted down Hamilton's tariff proposal.

The differences between Hamilton and Jefferson were profound, and the rift between the two men grew in the latter part of Washington's first term.

Hamilton recognized that the United States would have to concentrate on developing its own industry in order to achieve economic independence from Europe, where by the end of the 18th century the Industrial Revolution was in full swing. The invention of the cotton gin by Eli Whitney in 1793 contributed greatly to the American Industrial Revolution.

Washington at his beloved Virginia estate, Mount Vernon. Jefferson believed the cultivated, leisurely existence of the gentlemen planters of the Virginia aristocracy should serve as a model for the country's future development.

The tariff was merely one area of antagonism. Their quarrel resulted in part from dissimilarities in background and outlook and in part from clashing ambition. Americans of the 18th century were not comfortable with political infighting. In an age where political differences were feared as harbingers of "factionalism" — an evil deplored by most political thinkers of the day, including "Publius," the author of *The Federalist* — Hamilton and Jefferson both believed that nothing less than the fate of the young republic was at stake in their disagreement. Each saw the other as a diabolical schemer pursuing a political agenda for his own selfish ends. Although both feared the onset of factionalism, their feud — perhaps the most notorious in American political history — helped hasten the creation of the American party system.

Jefferson's mistrust of Hamilton dated to the Constitutional Convention. Although Jefferson supported the Constitution, he remained wary of the possibilities for tyranny inherent in a strong central government, and he worried that the Constitution could be used to deny individual liberties. For Hamilton, of course, the strength the Constitution invested the federal government with was its most laudable feature. While Hamilton increased the power of the federal government through the implementation of his fiscal policies, Jefferson remembered Hamilton's original proposals at the Constitutional Convention and suspected that Hamilton still harbored monarchist sympathies. Hamilton's early success as Treasury secretary further angered Jefferson, who saw his vision of America as a nation of self-sufficient gentleman farmers rapidly fading. Jefferson was appalled by the orgy of speculation and corruption that followed the introduction of Hamilton's plans, and he resented Washington's affection for Hamilton and his support of the Treasury secretary's policies. Neither man tolerated disagreement or rivals well. Both Hamilton and Jefferson were extremely ambitious, and each wished to be Washington's most trusted adviser and the preeminent member of the cabinet.

The sage of Monticello, Thomas Jefferson, hard at work on the Declaration of Independence. Jefferson and Hamilton were by far the most talented members of Washington's cabinet; the monumental ambition of each made it perhaps inevitable they would clash.

As the author of the Declaration of Independence, Jefferson was already known throughout the world, but he feared that he was being overshadowed by Hamilton. For his part, Hamilton believed that Jefferson was motivated solely by his desire for power, not by honest disagreement with the direction the government was taking. Neither was particularly sensitive about the other's sensibilities. Jefferson did not hesitate to attempt to influence the administration's economic strategy, and Hamilton thought nothing about interfering with the making of foreign policy — nominally Jefferson's area of responsibility.

Nowhere did the difference in outlook between the two men manifest itself more clearly than on foreign policy matters. Hamilton's passion for stability and order and his suspicion of democracy left him favorably inclined toward Great Britain. Jefferson had served as minister to France and believed that nation's assistance to the United States during the revolutionary war made it the new republic's most

A satanic observer (far left) chortles at the folly of the members of the "Antifederal Club" in this 1793 cartoon. The drawing portrays the members of Jefferson's party, also known as the Republicans, as a lawless rabble resentful of any government authority.

natural ally. Whereas Jefferson was impressed by the democratic principles expressed during the early days of the ongoing French Revolution (which drew much of its inspiration from the ideals contained in the Declaration of Independence), Hamilton was dismayed by the social upheaval and outbreaks of mob violence that accompanied the French uprising. The situation grew even more complicated with France's decision to carry its Revolution abroad as a struggle against Europe's monarchies and its declaration of war against Britain on February 1, 1793.

In the meantime, Jefferson and Madison had determined to drive Hamilton from office. Their followers had begun to organize and were referring to themselves as Democratic Republicans, or often just Republicans. Those who supported Hamilton and his policies called themselves Federalists, the name originally used by advocates of the Constitution.

John Fenno's *Gazette of the United States* was virtually the only newspaper of the day that provided extensive coverage of national politics. Fenno's

An unruly mob clamors for the head of King Louis XVI of France during the French Revolution. Jefferson had served as minister to France and was sympathetic to the Revolution's aims; Hamilton detested it.

Although Vice-president John Adams was a fellow Federalist, Hamilton disliked him almost as much as he did Jefferson. Adams, in turn, regarded Hamilton as little more than an ambitious schemer. Their feud would help destroy the Federalist party.

newspaper reflected his enthusiastic support of Hamilton's programs. Seeking an organ of their own, Jefferson and Madison persuaded Philip Freneau, who had won some renown for his patriotic poems during the revolutionary war, to found the *National Gazette*. Jefferson helped Freneau subsidize his endeavor by securing him a sinecure as a translator in the State Department. The *National Gazette* was first published on October 31, 1791, and soon became a forum for vituperative attacks on Hamilton, some penned by Madison. It was not long before the *Gazette of the United States* responded in kind.

Jefferson also used more direct tactics. In May 1792 he wrote a long letter to Washington in which he charged Hamilton with various misdeeds. Chief among them was Hamilton's using his economic policies to create a climate conducive to the type of frenzied speculation in securities, bonds, and paper money from which his friends and supporters among the moneyed interests in the Northeast were profiting. The result, as Jefferson saw it, was systematic corruption, "nourish[ing] in our people habits of vice and idleness, instead of industry and morality." Jefferson warned the president that the real intent of Hamilton's schemes was to effect "a change from the present republican form of government to that of a monarchy, of which the English Constitution is to be the model." Six weeks later Jefferson repeated his charges in a conversation with Washington, who dismissed his fears as groundless. The greatest danger to the republic, Washington said, came from the sort of irresponsible charges leveled by Freneau and his like, whose goal was to incite opposition to the government. As such attacks tended to create disunion and anarchy, the president admonished, it was no surprise that some advocated recourse to stronger governmental authority.

Hamilton was to some degree taken by surprise by the depths of the opposition to him. He was particularly hurt to discover that Madison, his former collaborator and ally, was now apparently an implacable enemy. In a May 1792 letter to Federalist

Edward Carrington, Hamilton attributed Madison's apostasy to Jefferson's hypnotic influence. Hamilton described Jefferson as the ringleader of a conspiracy that aimed to destroy the public credit, weaken the federal government, and lead the nation into war with Great Britain. Jefferson's motivation, Hamilton believed, was his desire to be president. When Washington offered Hamilton an opportunity to respond in writing to the charges Jefferson had made, Hamilton elaborated on his accusations. He felt that Jefferson was playing upon the public's fear of monarchy to advance his own ambition and alleged that the greatest danger to the republic came not from his own policies but from the type of demagoguery Jefferson was practicing: "The only path to a subversion of the republican system of the Country is by flattering the prejudices of the people, and exciting their jealousies and apprehensions, to throw affairs into confusion, and bring on civil commotion. Tired at length of anarchy, or want of government, they may take shelter in the arms of monarchy for repose and security."

Once on the offensive, Hamilton pursued his attack with characteristic energy, using Fenno's *Gazette of the United States* as his forum. He wrote a number of articles under various pseudonyms, outlining old charges — Jefferson opposed the Constitution and had obstructed attempts to restore the public credit — and new ones — Jefferson had misused government funds to establish Freneau's newspaper. Washington was unable to make peace between his two battling ministers, despite pointing out that dissension posed a particular threat to a government still trying to establish its legitimacy as a national authority. The only thing Hamilton and his primary antagonist were able to agree upon was that Washington should serve another term, and they persuaded the somewhat reluctant president to seek reelection. Washington again won unanimous election, with Massachusetts's John Adams as his vice-president, but Hamilton's support was waning. When the third Congress assembled in Philadelphia, Republicans controlled the majority of the seats.

[Jefferson] is crafty, not scrupulous about the means of success, not very mindful of truth.
—ALEXANDER HAMILTON

6

Prime Minister

France went to war with Austria and Prussia in April 1792. That November France's revolutionary government offered "fraternal assistance" to the continent's oppressed peoples, and the war soon consumed the rest of Europe. When Great Britain joined the fray in February 1793, the dispute between Hamilton and Jefferson regarding the United States's response became an issue of paramount importance.

Jefferson hastened to point out that by the terms of the treaties of assistance concluded with France during the revolutionary war, the United States was officially France's ally, committed to helping defend France's possessions in the West Indies. Although he regarded the French Revolution as "the most sacred cause that ever man was engaged in," Jefferson believed it behooved the United States to remain neutral in the European conflict. He recommended that the United States act impartially but avoid officially declaring a policy of neutrality. If the United States was unable to provide France with help, Jefferson argued, it could at least use the threat of support as a bargaining chip to force Britain into certain concessions, such as easing its restrictions on trade with the United States or removing the garrisons it had maintained in the new nation's Northwest Territory since the revolutionary war.

I am glad to believe there is no real resemblance between what was the cause of America and what is the cause of France— that the difference is no less great than that between liberty and licentiousness.
—ALEXANDER HAMILTON

Hamilton, as captured by the American artist John Trumbull in 1806. The portrait is now part of the permanent collection at the National Gallery in Washington, D.C.

Hamilton's support of Great Britain rested on practical considerations as well as philosophical affinity. Because Britain was the United States's most important trading partner and possessed the world's most powerful navy, it stood able to inflict serious damage upon the American economy should it so desire. Hamilton asserted that the U.S. treaties with France had been made with the French monarchy and became invalid when the Revolution overthrew King Louis XVI. The wise move, he told Washington, would be to declare neutrality immediately.

Napoleon Bonaparte leads French troops against Austrian forces at the Battle of Arcole in 1796. Revolutionary France's success on the battlefields of Europe emboldened it to step up its attacks on American shipping and demand greater concessions from American negotiators.

Despite the rift in his cabinet and the conflicting advice he was receiving, Washington was of a clear mind as to what course the United States should pursue. He harbored a suspicion of entangling alliances and feared the consequences should the United States involve itself in the European war. On April 22, 1793, Washington issued a proclamation of neutrality, which declared the United States to be "friendly and impartial toward the belligerent powers" and warned its citizens not to aid either nation. Without specifically abrogating the treaty with France, Washington essentially laid it aside.

The French ambassador to the United States, Citizen Edmond Genet, presents himself to Washington. Genet so overstepped the bounds of diplomatic propriety that even Jefferson, revolutionary France's greatest defender in the cabinet, concurred in the decision to petition for his recall.

Washington's decision did not end Britain's and France's efforts to enlist or coerce the support of the United States. No sooner had France's minister to the United States, Edmond Genet — known, in the democratic parlance of revolutionary France, as Citizen Genet — arrived than he set about commissioning privately owned American ships as privateers under the French flag, establishing his own courts to condemn British vessels seized by the privateers, and organizing western settlers into an invasion force for an attack on the Spanish city of New Orleans. He also made noise about future marches on Florida and Canada. Genet's antics tried even Jefferson's patience, and before long the cabinet voted unanimously to ask for his recall. France complied, but the Revolution had entered a bloody phase known as the Reign of Terror, and Genet feared that if he returned to his country the guillotine would be his fate, as it had been for thousands of his fellow citizens. He settled on the banks of the Hudson with the daughter of Governor Clinton instead.

Hamilton and the Federalists delighted in Genet's folly, but Great Britain was not winning new allies in the United States either. American merchants believed that the United States had the right to trade with all the belligerents in the war and were reluctant to cease their lucrative commerce with the French colonies in the West Indies. Britain responded by seizing American trading ships. The British governor-general of Canada, Lord Dorchester, provoked further enmity by encouraging the Creek Indians of the Ohio territory in their hostility toward American settlers.

The proclamation of neutrality was not unanimously well received. When Jefferson continued his lobbying on behalf of France, Hamilton wrote a series of newspaper articles defending the wisdom of Washington's decision and his constitutional authority to direct foreign policy. Madison responded to Jefferson's entreaty that he defend the Republican position, but the urgency of his plea aside — "For God's sake, my dear Sir, take up your pen, select the most striking heresies and cut him to pieces in face of the public" — Jefferson was losing his taste for politics. His most recent attempt to drive Hamilton from office had failed — in February a Jefferson-inspired congressional investigation into Hamilton's management of Treasury Department finances had revealed no impropriety — and the neutrality proclamation had again demonstrated Washington's partiality to Hamilton's counsel. On July 31, 1793, Jefferson offered Washington his resignation, effective at the end of the year.

What should have been Hamilton's moment of triumph found him weary, worn down by political squabbling and the attacks of his opponents. Like Jefferson before him and Washington at present, he craved retirement. But Washington depended on him now more than ever, and Jefferson's departure left him truly the "prime minister," without rival as the most powerful member of Washington's administration. Retirement would wait, but illness forced a temporary withdrawal from the concerns of office. In September 1793 Hamilton was felled by the yellow fever epidemic that claimed the lives of 5,000 Phi-

Maximilien Robespierre, dictator of France during the bloodiest period of the Reign of Terror, goes to the guillotine in 1794. The breakdown of authority in revolutionary France reaffirmed Hamilton's belief in strong central government.

A good Samaritan helps a victim of the Philadelphia yellow-fever epidemic of 1793 to a carriage that will take him to a hospital. Both Hamilton and his wife were stricken, but innovative medical care helped them to recover.

ladelphians that autumn. Elizabeth also was stricken. Fortunately, the Hamiltons' physician was Alexander's childhood friend Edward Stevens. He ignored the standard treatments of purges and bloodletting and instead prescribed bed rest, cold baths, and Madeira wine. The immediate crisis passed quickly, and the Hamiltons left Philadelphia for Albany, where they completed their recovery.

A weakened Hamilton was back at his desk by early December, only to discover that his opponents had used his time away to regroup. The war between Great Britain and France was again the issue. Britain had stepped up its seizures of American trading vessels. While Congress debated the wisdom of retaliatory measures aimed at British commerce — the proposals came from Madison, acting on Jefferson's parting recommendations — its more excitable members called for war with Britain. In response Hamilton prepared a speech to be delivered by William Loughton Smith of South Carolina, in which he demonstrated that despite the mother country's recent truculence, trade with Britain continued to be extremely advantageous for the United States. France was not in a position to bestow similar benefits. Hamilton pointed out that Britain provided 75 percent of American imports and was also the largest consumer of American trade goods. In addition Britain provided its American trading partners with liberal credit, freeing American capital for investment at home. Hamilton's address featured his usual devastating logic and impressive array of factual material and statistics, but Britain's assaults continued, amplified by Dorchester's incitement of the western Indians, and the Republicans continued to clamor for redress. They now advocated a halt to all dealings with Great Britain and a suspension of private debts owed by Americans to British merchants until Britain's behavior became more acceptable.

The suggestions appalled Hamilton, who believed they would lead to a war that would be certain to destroy the American economy and consequently the Union. He advised Washington as much, recommending a policy of intensive negotiation backed by military preparedness. In March 1794 the House of Representatives passed a resolution authorizing the establishment of the first American navy. Washington regarded his trusted Treasury secretary as the man best suited to head the diplomatic mission to England, but even Hamilton recognized that his appointment would result in a fire storm of controversy. Washington then considered John Adams and Jefferson before acceding to Hamilton's endorsement of his old friend and political ally John Jay: "Mr. Jay is the only man in whose qualifications for success there would be thorough confidence."

As ever, Hamilton's self-confidence was abundant, even, his critics charged, excessive. Edmund Randolph had replaced Jefferson as secretary of state, but Hamilton took it upon himself to prepare Jay for his mission. He charged Assistant Secretary of the Treasury Tench Coxe with tutoring Jay on Britain's economic history. Hamilton himself briefed Jay on the negotiating strategy to follow. He

In every relation which you have borne to me, I have found that my confidence in your talents, exertions, and integrity has been well placed.
—GEORGE WASHINGTON
to Alexander Hamilton

advised Jay to press for indemnification for losses suffered by American merchants due to the seizure of their ships, an end to Britain's arming and inciting of the Indians, settlement of unresolved disputes concerning the revolutionary war's peace treaty, and trade concessions. These were objectives that Republicans as well as Federalists agreed upon, but when Randolph added a few points of his own, Hamilton cautioned Jay about the dangers of inflexibility. Britain was much stronger than the United States, he warned. The benefits to be gained from successful negotiation were such that the United States should be willing to make concessions, and Jay should not risk failing to gain a treaty by insisting on points Britain would never concede. Once Jay had been dispatched, Hamilton took it upon himself to meet with the British minister and assure him that the United States had no intention of joining Denmark and Sweden in their policy of "armed neutrality." Republicans charged that Hamilton had undercut Jay's bargaining position, removing one of the few threats the United States could hold against the British. When Jay returned with a treaty that not only did not guarantee an end to British interference with American shipping but further restricted American trade with the West Indies and also forbade American traders from shipping molasses, sugar, coffee, cocoa, or cotton anywhere in the world, their howls of disapproval grew louder.

The Republicans kept Hamilton busy with domestic concerns as well. The earlier investigation of his management of the Treasury Department had resulted in Hamilton's complete vindication, but the Republicans continued to insist that there was something amiss in his handling of government funds. Congress initiated a new examination in the last month of 1793. Again Hamilton fully complied with each of Congress's requests for documents and material, even attending more than half of the investigatory sessions. Again nothing, aside from trivialities, was discovered, but the inquiry was extremely time-consuming and succeeded somewhat in keeping Hamilton on the defensive.

> *I have no reason to believe that a treaty more favorable to us is attainable.*
> —JOHN JAY

Hamilton considered letting Congress's exoneration serve as his farewell, but the counsel of friends and his still unflagging energy convinced him to stay on. Not content with attending to matters of the economy and foreign affairs, Hamilton turned his attention to the military. Finding Secretary of War Henry Knox insufficiently zealous in directing the construction of the navy and outfitting the troops of revolutionary war hero "Mad" Anthony Wayne for their upcoming offensive against the western Indians, Hamilton determined to undertake the supervision of those tasks.

A federal excise tax on whiskey had been one of Hamilton's ideas for raising revenue to retire the public debt. The tax had been opposed by southern and western farmers ever since Congress had approved it in March 1791. Resistance was greatest among the fiercely independent Scotch-Irish farmers of western Pennsylvania, who regarded virtually any exercise of the federal government's authority as a tyrannical imposition. Because it was more easily transported to seaboard markets than grain,

Merchant ships on the James River in Virginia are loaded with tobacco for transport to England. One reason Hamilton supported Great Britain so strongly was that he recognized that the American economy was not yet strong enough to withstand a break with its primary trading partner.

John Jay served in the Continental Congress and helped negotiate the Treaty of Paris, which ended the revolutionary war. He also served as secretary of foreign affairs under the Articles of Confederation, presided as first chief justice of the Supreme Court, negotiated Jay's Treaty with Great Britain, and was governor of New York.

whiskey was virtually a cash crop in western Pennsylvania. It was also universally accepted in the area for use in barter in lieu of cash. Western Pennsylvania's farmers and distillers regarded the whiskey tax as ample proof that Hamilton's policies were designed to enrich the eastern seaboard's merchants and opposed it with a vehemence akin to that displayed by the colonists to the stamp and tea taxes. Federal tax collectors were threatened, and some were tarred and feathered.

Hamilton took some steps to pacify the opposition. He lowered the excise on domestic spirits while raising the tax on imported ones. Washington issued a presidential proclamation calling for compliance. Opposition, in the form of nonpayment, continued, and attempts to bring offenders to court in the summer of 1794 were met with violence. Mobs shot at federal officials and destroyed the property of those who complied with the law. Protesters set fire to a tax collector's home. Vows of defiance were exclaimed at mass meetings. Steps were taken to organize a farmers' militia to march on the government fort at Pittsburgh. Resistance spread to Maryland.

Hamilton was convinced that the Whiskey Rebellion posed a threat to the Union itself. He saw the uprising not as opposition to a specific policy but as a violent denial of the federal government's authority to conduct its legitimate business. If the government failed to assert its authority, it could only expect further lawlessness in the future. He advised

Washington of the need for "an immediate resort to Military force." At issue were fundamental concepts that had been debated since the days of the Articles of Confederation. The question, he wrote Washington, was really a very simple one: "Shall the majority govern or be governed? Shall the nation rule, or be ruled? Shall the general will prevail, or the will of a faction?" Hamilton believed, he told Washington, "that mankind must have government of one sort or another." Government derived its authority from either rule of law or force. Democracy and constitutional government protected individual liberty precisely because they embodied and derived their authority from rule of law. In Hamilton's mind, failure to suppress the Whiskey Rebellion would be subversive of the authority upon which the Constitution was based and would lead the United States toward government by force. When the law is disobeyed, he counseled Washington, force "must be substituted; and where this becomes the ordinary instrument of government there is an end to liberty. Those, therefore, who preach doctrines, or set examples, which undermine or subvert the authority of the laws, lead us from freedom to slavery; they incapacitate us for a government of laws, and consequently prepare the way for one of force."

Washington concurred, declaring Pennsylvania's western counties to be in "open rebellion" and calling for Pennsylvania, Maryland, New Jersey, and Virginia to muster militias. Both Hamilton and Washington hoped that a show of strength would quiet the rebels, but the unrest continued. Convinced that his own participation would render the operation less inflammatory, Washington assumed personal command of the 15,000-strong force. Hamilton, who was now also the acting secretary of war, persuaded Washington to let him accompany the expedition on the grounds that it was his department and policies the rebellion was focused against. He also argued that as the chief advocate of military action he should share in any direct danger resulting from the implementation of that policy.

The first secretary of war of the United States, Henry Knox. His heroism during the revolutionary war endeared him to Washington, who made him the youngest major general in the Continental Army. He succeeded Washington as commander in chief in 1784.

Hamilton left Philadelphia for the west with the president on September 30, 1794. Washington returned to the capital after three weeks, leaving Henry Lee of Virginia in charge of the troops but Hamilton in command of the entire operation. Armed resistance melted away, but Hamilton, with Washington's blessing, had 150 of the rebellion's alleged leaders arrested. Two were ultimately convicted of treason; Washington pardoned both. By the middle of November, Hamilton was on his way back to Philadelphia. Washington was hailed for the combination of strength and mercy with which he had handled the rebellion, and supporters of the administration won a majority in Congress in the elections shortly afterward. Hamilton delighted in the success of the military campaign—"A large army has cooled the courage of these madmen," he wrote, "and the only question now seems to be how to guard against the return of the phrenzy" — but he did not enjoy Washington's personal popularity and was roundly criticized for his role in suppressing the uprising. Familiar charges — Hamilton was a

Having tarred and feathered a tax official and burned his family out of their home, some western Pennsylvania farmers, angered by the government's enforcement of a tax on distilled spirits, prepare to inflict further punishment on their unfortunate victim.

Elizabeth Hamilton. Although Hamilton engaged in a well-publicized extramarital affair, his letters to his wife suggest that their relationship was warm and affectionate.

monarchist, an aristocrat, an enricher of the wealthy at the expense of the poor — were mingled with new allegations that Hamilton was a would-be dictator, unwilling to brook dissent, who would ride at the head of an army to deprive farmers of their right to opposition.

Believing the government and the nation to be stronger for his counsel, Hamilton was ready to take his leave of office, as is evident in a letter he wrote to his sister-in-law in December of 1794: "All is well with the public. Our insurrection is most happily terminated. Government has gained by it reputation and strength, and our finances are in a most flourishing condition. Having contributed to place those of the nation on a good footing, I go to take a little care of my own; which need my care not a little." He had more than financial concerns; Elizabeth had recently suffered a miscarriage and was gravely ill, as was one of their sons. Hamilton announced his resignation on December 1, 1794.

7

Affairs of State

Government service had not been financially rewarding for Hamilton. His meager annual salary had forced him to accept financial help from his father-in-law in order to maintain his family's accustomed standard of living, and he discovered upon return to private life that his debts far outnumbered his assets. Although Philip Schuyler was gracious and generous in aiding his daughter's growing family — by that time the Hamiltons had five children — Hamilton's pride would not allow him to remain dependent upon such an arrangement. After a lengthy vacation in Albany the family again took up residence in New York City, where Hamilton reestablished his legal practice. Before long he numbered among his clientele, in the words of his grandson and biographer, Allan McLane Hamilton, "nearly every one of wealth and influence in New York," and his income quadrupled his salary as Treasury secretary. But like his adversary Jefferson, Hamilton could not remain uninvolved with national concerns.

[Hamilton] worked for the peace, prosperity, and freedom of the entire community. His client was not a class but the country.
—BROADUS MITCHELL
Hamilton biographer

Hamilton's departure from office in 1794 did not lessen his involvement in the public affairs of the nation. He continued to advise Washington on virtually every issue affecting the administration.

John Jay is burned in effigy. Jay's Treaty with Great Britain in 1794 infuriated many Americans, particularly the Republicans, who believed it contained unacceptable concessions.

John Jay returned from England with his treaty in March 1794. Rumors of its terms had been circulating for months and had already sparked fierce dispute; Jay's arrival touched off controversy the likes of which the young nation had not seen. Opponents of the treaty denounced it as an abject surrender of America's sovereignty. Defenders appraised it as a realistic compromise that kept the United States out of war with Britain. An angry mob attacked the home of the British minister in Philadelphia. Jay was hung in effigy and condemned as a traitor. Hamilton was stoned in the streets of New York. Newspapers debated the merits and failings of the treaty.

The Republicans were in the forefront of the opposition to the treaty. Hamilton was no longer in government, but he was still recognized as the most important Federalist. He sought to rally public opinion in favor of the treaty by penning, with assistance from Jay and New York senator Rufus King, 38 lengthy essays that appeared in the New York *Argus* and elsewhere under the pen name "Camillus." The Camillus essays depicted Jay's Treaty as a skillful balancing of mutual concessions. Hamilton conceded that Britain's stands on several issues — impressment of American sailors, trade with the West Indies — were unwise but argued that overall the treaty was a fair one and kept the United States from war. The Senate had already advised Washington to ratify the treaty, with the stipulation that the noxious West Indian trade clause was not agreed to, but the Republican majority in the House of Representatives voted to refuse to appropriate funds necessary to carry out the treaty. Hamilton persuaded his followers to deluge the House with petitions in favor of the treaty. The Republican majority gave way in the face of Hamilton's orchestration of public opinion, and the House approved the appropriations on April 29, 1796.

The bitterly partisan debate surrounding Jay's Treaty helped strengthen Washington's determination to retire from politics at the conclusion of his second term. He intended his valedictory address to be a summation of the nation's progress under his leadership and a warning of pitfalls and perils still to come. Madison had drafted a farewell address for the president four years earlier, near the conclusion of Washington's first term; the president since had made many revisions. He now sent the entire document to Hamilton for editing, or, if Hamilton deemed it necessary, "to throw the whole into a different form."

Hamilton welcomed the freedom to rework the address and spent two and a half months in the summer of 1796 on his own draft, working, in his wife's words, "principally at such times as his Office was seldom frequented by his clients and visitors, and during the absence of his students to avoid interruption." Hamilton's ability to translate the president's ideas into prose made him particularly well-suited for the task. Washington's Farewell Address, destined to become one of the best known speeches in American history, was essentially Hamilton's "Original Major Draft." Perhaps one-half of that document originated with Hamilton; the rest was derived from Madison and Washington's earlier work. Hamilton's hand was clearly evident in the major theme of the address — the continuing danger posed to the Union by sectional and party disputes and "the insidious wiles of foreign influence."

The sharp criticism and scorn heaped on [Jay's] treaty by Republican editors sparked a popular furor that had not been matched since the violent days of Tory witch hunts during the Revolution.
—JACOB E. COOKE
Hamilton biographer

John Adams's presidency was a disappointment in comparison with his earlier triumphs as a leader of the revolutionary cause and a diplomat to Europe. His signing of the Alien and Sedition Acts, which prohibited written or spoken criticism of the government, is usually cited as his greatest mistake.

Washington's departure left Hamilton somewhat at sea. He had grown accustomed to advising the president on virtually every aspect of government, a practice that had continued, at Washington's insistence, even after Hamilton's ostensible retirement. Hamilton was the most important Federalist, but even he recognized that he was unsuitable as a presidential candidate. The Federalist candidate for president in the election of 1796 was John Adams. His Republican opponent was Thomas Jefferson. Both candidates righteously denounced factionalism and maintained an aloof distance from the campaign, but the election was clearly a partisan contest.

Relations between the debonair Hamilton and the stern, dour Adams had always been cool at best, despite a shared admiration for the British constitution and distaste for the French Revolution. Much about Hamilton, from his finely tailored clothes, to his air of supreme self-confidence and reputation as a flirt, annoyed Adams and his wife, Abigail. Adams resented the acclaim Hamilton had achieved and his influence on Washington. Somewhat pompous and vain, Adams believed that his own contributions to the birth of the new nation had been overlooked.

Hamilton was not enamored of Adams, but he detested Jefferson. Under the system for electing the president originally enacted under the Constitution, each elector cast two ballots. The candidate who received the most ballots would be president; the candidate with the second most, vice-president. Hamilton's goal in the election was to keep Jefferson out of government. A canvass of electors told him that Adams was likely to win the presidency; what Hamilton feared was that southern Federalist electors, out of regional loyalty, would name Jefferson on one of their ballots, thereby enabling Jefferson to win the vice-presidency. To offset this, Hamilton secured the nomination of South Carolinian Thomas Pinckney as the Federalist vice-presidential candidate — hoping thereby to appeal to the regionalism of southern Republicans, on the chance that some would desert their party's candidate for vice-president, the New Yorker Aaron Burr — and urged New England Federalists to name Adams and Pinckney on both of their ballots. The possibility that his maneuvering would lead to Pinckney's being elected president did not dismay Hamilton, as he recognized Adams's independence of mind and believed that Pinckney would be infinitely more receptive to his advice.

Hamilton's strategy did not work. Adams received 71 votes and became president; Jefferson, with 68, became vice-president. Pinckney received 58 votes. Adams was among those who believed that Hamilton had intrigued to deny him the presidency. Abigail Adams drew the same conclusion and warned her husband against Hamilton's scheming. She described him in a letter to her husband as "ambitious as Julius Caesar, a subtle intriguer . . . I have ever kept my eye upon him." Adams replied that he had long been on his guard against Hamilton, whom he regarded as "a proud, spirited, conceited, aspiring mortal . . . with as debauched morals as old [Benjamin] Franklin." On another occasion he characterized Hamilton as the "bastard brat of a Scotch pedlar."

> *All personal and partial considerations must be discarded, and everything must give way to the great object of excluding Jefferson.*
> —ALEXANDER HAMILTON
> on the election of 1796

> " The House refumed the confideration of the re-
> " port of the Committee, to whom was referred the
> " memorial of Andrew G. Fraunces : whereupon,
>
> " *Refolved*, That the reafons affigned by the fecre-
> " tary of the treafury, for refufing payment of the
> " warrants referred to in the memorial, are fully
> " fufficient to juftify his conduct ; and that in the
> " whole courfe of this tranfaction, the fecretary and
> " other officers of the treafury, have acted a meri-
> " torious part towards the public."
>
> " *Refolved*, That the charge exhibited in the me-
> " morial, againft the fecretary of the treafury, rela-
> " tive to the purchafe of the penfion of Baron de
> " Glaubeck is wholly illiberal and groundlefs*."

Was it not to have been expected that thefe repeated demonftrations of the injuftice of the accufations hazarded againft me would have abafhed the enterprife of my calumniators? However natural fuch an expectation may feem, it would betray an ignorance of the true character of the Jacobin fyftem. It is a maxim deeply ingrafted in that dark fyftem, that no character, however upright, is a match for conftantly reiterated attacks, however falfe. It is well underftood by its difciples, that every calumny makes fome profelites and even retains fome ; fince juftification feldom circulates as rapidly and as widely as flander. The number of thofe who from doubt proceed to fufpicion and thence to belief of imputed guilt is continually augmenting ; and the public mind fatigued at length with refiftance to the calumnies which eternally affail it, is apt in the end to fit down with the opinion that a perfon fo often accufed cannot be entirely innocent.

A paragraph from a 95-page pamphlet Hamilton wrote and had published in 1796, detailing his affair with Maria Reynolds. Hamilton was willing to admit to adultery if it would allay accusations of financial misconduct.

Despite his vigilance, Adams was unable to keep Hamilton away from affairs of state. He kept all four of Washington's cabinet officers on, and they continued to solicit Hamilton's advice. Adams was particularly enraged when Hamilton interceded regarding the United States's relations with France, which had replaced Britain as the chief nemesis of American shipping. Jay's Treaty marked a turning point in U.S.-British relations, but Britain and France remained at war, and France had announced that it considered itself within its rights to seize American ships engaged in trade with or bearing products from any of its many enemies. With French privateers regularly seizing American vessels, American envoys to France receiving insulting treatment, and firebrands in Congress calling for war, Hamilton counseled patience, conciliation, and negotiation. He even recommended that Jefferson and Madison be sent as members of a three-man diplomatic team to France. Although doctrinaire Federalists were enraged by Hamilton's attitude, he wrote in response, "We seem now to feel & reason as [we] did when Great Britain insulted and injured us, though certainly we have at least as much need of a temperate conduct now as we had then. I only say, God grant, that the public interest may not be sacrificed at the shrine of irritation and mistaken pride." Moderation and seeming good sense aside, Adams was infuriated by Hamilton's presumption in prescribing administration policy without being asked. Years later Adams wrote that he thought Hamilton must have been "in a delirium" at the time.

By the summer of 1797 Hamilton had more personal concerns. In July a disreputable journalist, James Callender, published allegations that during his time as Treasury secretary Hamilton had used one James Reynolds as an agent in carrying out private financial speculations reputed to have gained him enormous profits. He included documents demonstrating a financial relationship between Hamilton and Reynolds. Hamilton found the allegation of official impropriety unbearable, so much so that he was willing to confess to the sexual peccadillo that was at the root of the matter. The financial documents Callender had printed were receipts for blackmail money Hamilton had payed Reynolds. As Hamilton described it in the 95-page *mea culpa* he wrote and had published that summer, Reynolds's wife, Maria, came to Hamilton's Philadelphia home one afternoon in the summer of 1791 professing kinship with several prominent New York families known to Hamilton and telling a sad tale of abandonment by her husband. She then asked for a loan to return to New York. Hamilton promised to bring it to her that evening at her home, where he succumbed to temptation. The relationship continued, and after several months James Reynolds arrived on the scene, professing outrage

Hamilton manifestly found Maria an enchantress whose sexual spell kept him in thralldom, for he continued the liaison long after an iota of discretion would have warned him of its danger.
—JACOB E. COOKE
Hamilton biographer

and demanding money to keep quiet. Hamilton complied, continued the affair for several more months — it seemed he was unable to see that Maria was in cahoots with her husband — and then broke it off. When Reynolds wound up in jail months later on a fraud charge, he tried to force Hamilton to intercede on his behalf by claiming that he had been partners with the Treasury secretary in illegal speculation. Three congressmen, including future president James Monroe of Virginia, discreetly investigated the charges at that time and found them groundless. Hamilton's confession did not convince anyone who already believed him corrupt, and it could not have failed to hurt his wife, who nonetheless quickly forgave him. The affair also brought Hamilton to the brink of a duel with Monroe, who infuriated him by refusing to reiterate his earlier conviction of the propriety of Hamilton's official conduct. Hamilton was also wrongfully convinced that Monroe was responsible for leaking the documents to Callender.

The U.S. *Constellation* does battle with a French vessel, *L'Insurgent*, in February 1799. Repeated French attacks on American shipping had led to an undeclared naval war between the two nations.

In 1799 Napoleon Bonaparte (center), the hero of military campaigns against Austria and Britain, overthrew France's ruling Directory and installed himself as dictator. Napoleon's accession briefly eased hostilities between France and the United States.

While Hamilton was busy trying to clear his name, relations with France again worsened. Adams had dispatched a three-man negotiating team consisting of Pinckney, Elbridge Gerry, and John Marshall to France. Shortly after their arrival they met with representatives of the French foreign minister, Charles Talleyrand. These emissaries — identified in diplomatic dispatches only as X, Y, and Z — informed the Americans that a personal bribe equivalent to $250,000 was required in order to speak with Talleyrand and that nothing less than a loan of $6 million to the French government would end French attacks on American shipping. The affronted American delegation returned home, except for Gerry, who endured several more months of insults before leaving. Congress was outraged and repudiated all existing treaties with France, banned commerce between the two nations, authorized American ships to fight back when attacked, and allocated funds for the construction of naval vessels. An undeclared naval war broke out.

Hamilton essentially agreed with the measures, but he advised restraint backed with military preparedness. He was most interested in Congress's decision to strengthen the army and wished to be appointed inspector general, which would make him responsible for actually organizing the new forces. Adams, had he had his way, probably would have denied Hamilton any position at all, but he had immediately turned to Washington to serve as commander-in-chief and Washington had insisted on Hamilton's appointment. Even worse, from Adams's point of view, was Washington's stipulation that he would not become active unless "it becomes indispensable by the urgency of circumstances." Washington intended to remain essentially a figurehead; Hamilton would be in active command. There followed intrigue by Adams to appoint a general to outrank Hamilton, but Washington stood fast in his insistence that Hamilton be made the army's ranking officer, and Adams did not dare cross him.

I will never send another minister to France without assurances that he will be received, respected, and honored as the representative of a free, powerful, and independent nation.

—JOHN ADAMS
in reaction to the
XYZ affair

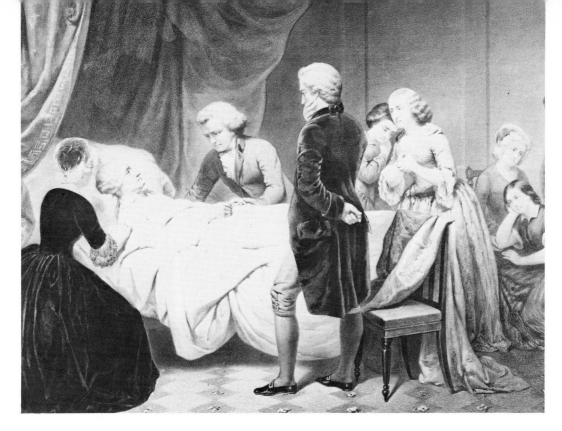

Hamilton's service as inspector general proved anticlimactic and unsuccessful. The immediate threat of war with France subsided with further peace overtures from Adams and the overthrow of France's ruling Directory by Napoleon Bonaparte. Hamilton believed that the new army could put a permanent end to the French threat by marching on Florida and Louisiana, which he knew Napoleon wished to obtain from Spain as the beginning of a North American empire. The plan had the additional virtue of appealing to the restless settlers of Virginia and Kentucky's western frontiers, who were angered by Spanish restrictions on navigation of the Mississippi and had been threatening secession and their own move on Louisiana for some time. But without the danger of immediate war with France as an impetus, Hamilton was unable to assemble the army he envisioned. Americans were still wary of the dangers of standing armies, recruits were few, and his plans dissolved amidst political squabbling and financial mismanagement.

The death of Washington, in December 1799. Hamilton wrote to Washington's wife, Martha: "From a calamity which is common to a mourning nation, who can expect to be exempt? Perhaps it is a privilege to have a claim to a larger portion of it than others."

8

"An Odd Destiny"

In opting for peace with France, Adams had placed himself in a difficult position for the 1800 elections, for his stand infuriated his own party, the Federalists. Although Adams was popular with the public, less than 40 percent of the electors in the 1800 presidential contest would be chosen by popular vote. The remainder would be selected by the state legislatures. New York's vote seemed likely to prove crucial in the presidential contest. Hamilton's longtime political rival Aaron Burr had taken charge of the Republican party there. (Like Hamilton, Burr was one of New York's foremost attorneys, but he was untrustworthy with money and teetered constantly at the edge of bankruptcy. He first won elective office by defeating Philip Schuyler, Hamilton's father-in-law, for the Senate in 1791.) Possessed of immense charm, tremendous organizing ability, and few scruples, Burr put together an extremely impressive slate of candidates to represent New York City for election to the state House of Representatives, then worked 10-hour days organizing precinct captains in every electoral district to ensure that Republican voters got to the polls on election day. His reward was a Republican victory, Republican control of the state legislature and selection of the state's presidential electors, and a place on the Republican ticket as the vice-presidential candidate.

[Aaron Burr was] the
Mephistopheles of Politics.
—HENRY ADAMS
American historian

Hamilton's injudicious attack on his own party's presidential candidate, John Adams, backfired, essentially ending his political career. In retirement he founded a newspaper and rebuilt his law practice.

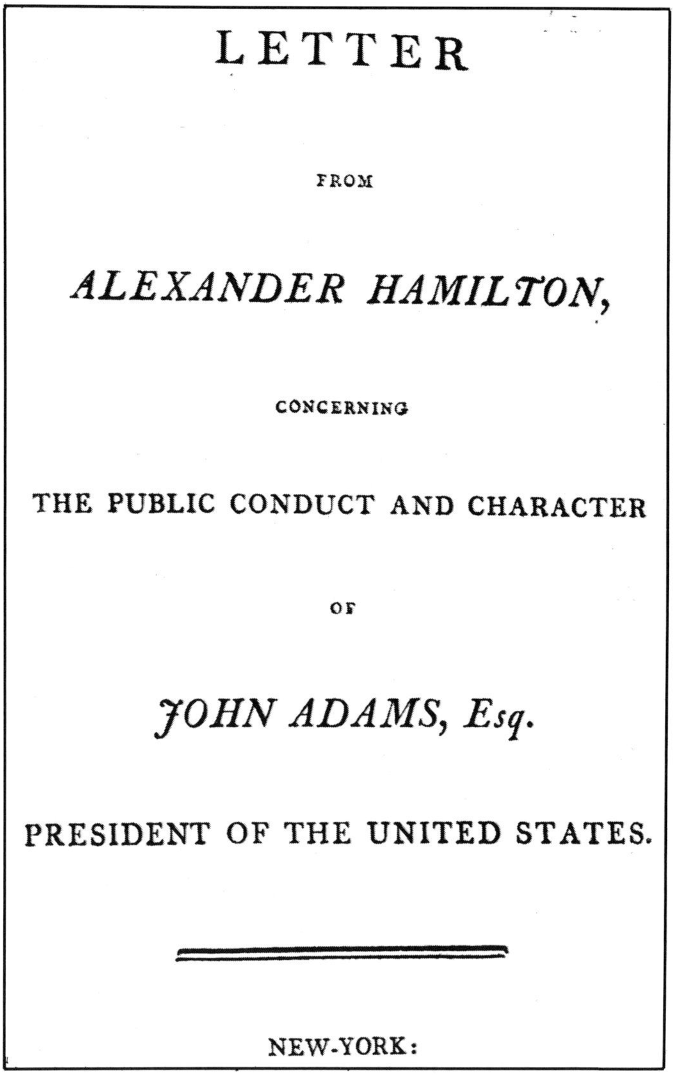

LETTER

FROM

ALEXANDER HAMILTON,

CONCERNING

THE PUBLIC CONDUCT AND CHARACTER

OF

JOHN ADAMS, Esq.

PRESIDENT OF THE UNITED STATES.

═══════════════

NEW-YORK:

The title page from a printed version of Hamilton's attack on Adams. For years it was believed that the letter was intended only for private circulation and was published at the initiative of Aaron Burr, who recognized the harm it would do the Federalists. More recent scholarship suggests Hamilton himself condoned publication.

Hamilton did not intend to campaign for Adams's reelection, but with Jefferson again the opposition party's nominee, he could not tolerate the prospect of a Republican victory. Hamilton hated Jefferson, and, though he had always gotten along personally with Burr, he considered him an amoral demagogue. He proposed to Governor John Jay that the outgoing legislature change the law to provide for popular election of presidential electors, hoping to negate Republican control of the incoming legislature. "In times like these in which we live," Hamilton wrote, "it will not do to be overscrupulous. It is easy to sacrifice the substantial interests of society by a strict adherence to ordinary rules." Hamilton had advocated popular election of electors for some time, but in the present context the plan appeared to be little more than a cheap campaign trick. Jay refused to countenance Hamilton's suggestion, dismissing the proposal as "a measure for party purposes which it would not become me to adopt."

Adams blamed Hamilton for the New York debacle, believing that he had somehow engineered the Federalists' defeat, and responded by dismissing from his cabinet Secretary of War James McHenry and Secretary of State Timothy Pickering, both Federalist supporters of Hamilton. It appeared Hamilton had been outmaneuvered. He disliked (and was disliked by) the incumbent president, who was his party's nominee, and the opposition's candidates were his implacable enemies. His solution was to secure the nomination of Charles Cotesworth Pinckney of South Carolina as the Federalist nominee for vice-president. As in 1796, it was still possible that a vice-presidential candidate could receive the most electoral votes and wind up as president. Hamilton aimed to persuade Federalist electors in New England to support Adams and Pinckney equally while convincing southern Federalists to abandon Adams and name Pinckney on one of their two ballots.

The campaign was notable for its use of denigrating rhetoric. The Federalists regularly equated the Republicans with the Jacobins, the party in revolutionary France responsible for the Reign of Terror, and warned voters that the safety of their homes, loved ones, and nation was at stake in the upcoming election. Jefferson was constantly denounced as an atheist. Republican propaganda was no more measured. James Callender pronounced Adams a "repulsive pedant, a gross hypocrite . . . and in private life one of the most egregious fools upon the continent . . . a wretch, that has neither the science of a magistrate, the politeness of a courtier, nor the courage of a man."

Hamilton helped secure the vice-presidential nomination for South Carolinian Charles Cotesworth Pinckney in 1800, then schemed to have Pinckney elected president instead of Adams or Jefferson. Four years earlier he had attempted a similar maneuver with Pinckney's younger brother Thomas.

Hamilton's archenemy Aaron Burr. Hamilton wrote of him in 1800: "There is nothing in his favor. His private character is not defended by his most partial friends. He is bankrupt beyond redemption except by the plunder of his country. His public principles have no other spring or aim than his own aggrandisement."

The atmosphere was conducive to Hamilton's machinations. When word reached him in June 1800 that Adams had accused him of heading a pro-British faction, Hamilton let loose his own invective. Addressed initially to prominent Federalists whom Hamilton wished to inform "of the facts which denote unfitness in Mr. Adams" for the presidency, Hamilton's missive, entitled *Letter from Alexander Hamilton Concerning the Public Conduct and Character of John Adams*, was subsequently printed and widely circulated. The diatribe was devoid of Hamilton's customary deliberate reasoning. It catalogued a long list of Adams's mistakes and failings as evidence of fundamental character flaws that included an "imagination sublimated and eccentric, propitious neither to the regular display of sound judgment nor to steady perseverance in a systematic plan of conduct"; "vanity without bounds, and a jealousy capable of discoloring every object"; "disgusting egoism"; and "ungovernable discretion of temper." The Republicans delighted in Hamilton's work, but his Federalist followers found it an unseemly display, certain to further divide the party. The prominent Federalist and lexicographer Noah Webster spoke for many in his party when he told Hamilton that "your ambition, pride and overbearing temper have destined you to be the evil genius of this country. Your conduct on this occasion will be deemed little short of insanity." The incident marked the end of Hamilton's influence as a political leader. Hamilton's friend Robert Troup wrote of the Adams letter that "an opinion has grown out of it, which at present obtains almost universally, that his [Hamilton's] character is *radically deficient in discretion* , and therefore the federalists ask, what avail the most preeminent talents — the most distinguished patriotism — without the all important quality of discretion?"

Going into the election the Federalists enjoyed a clear majority in both houses of Congress, but Hamilton's want of discretion helped destroy them as a viable political party. Adams polled 65 electoral votes and Pinckney 64, but Jefferson and Burr each received 73. The deadlocked election was thrown to the House of Representatives, where Jefferson won on the 36th ballot. Although his influence had diminished, Hamilton tirelessly implored Federalist legislators to vote for Jefferson, whom he now regarded as the lesser of two evils. Burr, Hamilton advised his correspondents, was the "most unfit and dangerous man of the Community," the quintessential demagogue whose "public principles have no other spring or aim than his own aggrandisement."

With Jefferson's inauguration, Hamilton had little choice but to accept that his political career was finished. He tried to make the best of his forced retirement. His law practice prospered, and he had a beautiful house in New York, called the Grange (named for the Hamilton family home in Scotland), built on a 30-acre tract overlooking the Hudson River, but Hamilton never adjusted to his new life. Accustomed to expressing his opinions, Hamilton founded a newspaper, the *New York Evening Post*, in November 1801. Hamilton's editor, William Coleman, explained how editorial policy was determined: "Whenever anything occurs on which I feel the want of information, I state the matter to him [Hamilton], sometimes in a note. He appoints a time when I may see him . . . [and] begins in a deliberate manner to dictate, and I to take down in short hand; when he stops my article is completed." The *Evening Post*'s opening editorial promised a moderate viewpoint: "Though we openly profess our attachment to that system of politics denominated Federal, because we think it most conducive to the welfare of the community . . . we . . . believe that honest and virtuous men are to be found in each party."

Yet the bitterness engendered by the partisan quarrels of the recent past would return to haunt Hamilton. Four days after the *Evening Post* began publishing, Hamilton's eldest son, 20-year-old Philip, was involved in a dispute with a Republican lawyer, George Eacker, regarding an anti-Federalist speech Eacker had given some months before.

Hamilton's oldest son, Philip, was killed in a duel in November 1801 occasioned by a political dispute. Hamilton's grief at his son's death was boundless.

Thomas Jefferson signs papers approving the purchase of the Louisiana Territory from France. The Louisiana Purchase more than doubled the size of the United States and freed the entire Mississippi River to American navigation.

Eacker challenged Philip to a duel, which ended with Philip mortally wounded. Hamilton was devastated by the death of the son he termed "the eldest and *brightest* hope of my family." That Philip's death had resulted in part from defending his father's honor only added to Hamilton's sorrow. He almost fainted at his son's funeral and had to be led from the church on the arms of friends. The tragedy did not end with Philip's death. Angelica, Hamilton's eldest daughter and the child closest to Philip, slipped into madness shortly thereafter and never recovered her sanity.

Hamilton was engulfed in despair. "Never did I see a man so completely overwhelmed with grief as Hamilton has been," Robert Troup wrote at that time. In earlier years he no doubt would have thrown himself into work as a restorative, but the endeavor that he loved best was no longer available to him. His country no longer had need of his singular gifts. "Mine is an odd destiny," he wrote Gouverneur Morris in February 1802. "Perhaps no man in the United States has sacrificed or done more for the present Constitution than myself—and contrary to all my anticipations of its fate . . . I am still labouring to prop the frail and worthless fabric. Yet I have the murmurs of its friends no less than the curses of its foes for my rewards. What can I do better than withdraw from the Scene? Every day proves to me more and more that this American world was not made for me."

Still, the American world exerted its pull. Hamilton continued to follow and comment on public affairs. He was virtually the only prominent Federalist to support Jefferson regarding the Louisiana Purchase, although he believed the same result could have been achieved less expensively through force of arms. Hamilton no doubt took satisfaction in knowing that the constitutional authority Jefferson claimed in order to acquire the Louisiana territory derived from his own broad constructionist interpretation of the Constitution.

He remained one of the nation's foremost attorneys and in one of his last cases established an important principle that helped safeguard freedom of the press. The case concerned Harry Croswell, editor of a small upstate New York newspaper, who asserted in print that Jefferson had paid the journalist James Callender to attack Washington, Adams, and other public figures. Croswell's allegation was accurate, but under the law of the day he still could be (and was) convicted of libel. Hamilton took

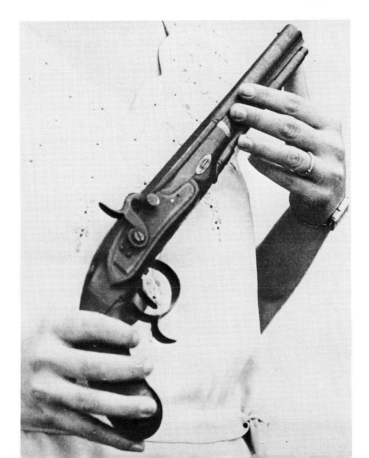

The pistol used by Aaron Burr to kill Alexander Hamilton.

Hamilton's statue outside the Treasury Department. The inscription reads, "First Secretary of the Treasury, Soldier, Orator, Statesman, Champion of Constitutional Union, Representative Government, and National Integrity."

the case on appeal and demonstrated the dubious origin of the English common-law doctrine that held truth to be no defense to libel. With virtually every member of the state legislature in attendance to hear his argument, Hamilton avowed that in a democracy truth must be a defense, for only in that way could a vigorous and free press — essential to the health of the republic — be guaranteed: "It is evident that if you cannot apply this mitigated doctrine for which I speak, to the case of libels here, you must forever remain ignorant of what your rulers do. I can never think this ought to be; I never did think the truth was a crime; I am glad the day is come in which it is to be decided; for my soul has ever abhorred the thought, that a free man dared not speak the truth." Hamilton lost the case, but although he did not convince the court, he convinced the legislature. The following year, 1805, a bill making truth a defense to libel was enacted as New York State law. In time the principle became a fundamental tenet of American law.

Vice-president Aaron Burr had been flirting with the Federalists since 1800, when the Federalists in the House cast their ballots for him rather than Jefferson in breaking the tie election. Enraged by the Louisiana Purchase, which they believed Jefferson wished to carve into several slaveholding states in order to ensure the South's political dominance, a group of northern Federalists, led by Washington's former secretary of state, Timothy Pickering, hatched a scheme to persuade the New England states to secede from the Union and form a separate nation. They regarded New York's support as essential to their cause. Hamilton summarily rebuffed their overtures, but in Burr they found their man. He agreed to run, with Federalist backing, for governor of New York. Hamilton worked to persuade his fellow Federalists to support the Republican candidate for governor. Burr was soundly routed, but Hamilton's sadly diminished influence was evident in the fact that more than 80 percent of the state's Federalists voted for Burr.

On June 18, 1804, Burr's close friend William Van Ness arrived at Hamilton's home and demanded an explanation for a recent newspaper article in which Hamilton was quoted as saying that "he looked upon Mr. Burr to be a dangerous man, and one who ought not to be trusted with the reins of government." The columnist then told his readers, "I could detail to you a still more despicable opinion which General HAMILTON has expressed of Mr. BURR." Although Hamilton's comment was somewhat mild in comparison with his past excoriations of Burr, Van Ness's language and the code of the day left little doubt that in lieu of an apology Hamilton would be challenged to a duel. Hamilton had abhorred dueling even before the custom had claimed the life of his son, but he did not feel he could apologize. In a document he wrote explaining his decision, Hamilton said that "what men of the world denominate honor" was at stake. He clung to a vision of future service to his country and believed that his "ability to be in future useful, whether in resisting mischief or in effecting good, in those crises of our public affairs, which seem likely to happen . . . would probably be inseparable from a conformity with public prejudice on this matter." Although he would participate in the duel, Hamilton had no intention of killing Burr. He would either intentionally miss or hold his fire.

The duel was scheduled for July 11. For the next two weeks Hamilton put his affairs in order, drafting a will and composing numerous farewell letters. He did not tell his wife about the impending confrontation. To all he appeared serene. He spent the night of July 10 writing a final letter to Elizabeth, concluding with "Adieu best of wives and best of women, embrace all my children for me. Ever yours." That night he slept beside his 13-year-old son. He awoke before dawn and was rowed shortly afterward across the Hudson River to Weehawken, New Jersey. Just after 7:00 A.M. Aaron Burr took careful aim, fired his pistol, and mortally wounded Alexander Hamilton. He "expired without a struggle" at his home some 31 hours later. The announcement of his death was followed by an outpouring of national grief unmatched since the death of George Washington five years earlier.

> *[Hamilton had the] touch of the heroic, the touch of the purple, the touch of the gallant, the dashing, the picturesque.*
> —THEODORE ROOSEVELT

Further Reading

Bruns, Roger. *George Washington.* New York: Chelsea House, 1987.

Cooke, Jacob E. *Alexander Hamilton.* New York: Scribners, 1982.

Daniels, Jonathan. *Ordeal of Ambition: Jefferson, Hamilton, Burr.* New York: Doubleday, 1970.

Emery, Noemie. *Alexander Hamilton.* New York: Putnam, 1982.

Flexner, James Thomas. *The Young Hamilton: A Biography.* Boston: Little, Brown, 1978.

Hacker, Louis Morton. *Alexander Hamilton in the American Tradition.* New York: McGraw-Hill, 1964.

Hamilton, Alexander. *The Papers of Alexander Hamilton.* 26 vols. Edited by Harold C. Syrett. New York: Columbia University Press, 1961–79.

Hamilton, James A. *Reminiscences.* New York: Scribners, 1869.

Hendrickson, Robert, *Hamilton.* Vol. 1 *1957–1789.* New York: Mason/Charter, 1976.

———. *Hamilton.* Vol. 2 *1789–1804.* New York: Mason/Charter, 1976.

———. *The Rise and Fall of Alexander Hamilton.* New York: Van Nostrand Reinhold, 1981.

Knight, Ralph. *The Burr-Hamilton Duel, July 11, 1804.* New York: Franklin Watts, 1968.

Lodge, Henry Cabot. *Alexander Hamilton.* New York: Chelsea House, 1980.

McDonald, Forrest. *Alexander Hamilton: A Biography.* New York: Norton, 1979.

Miller, John C. *Alexander Hamilton: Portrait in Paradox.* New York: Harper & Row, 1959.

Mitchell, Broadus. *Alexander Hamilton, Youth to Maturity 1755–1788.* New York: Macmillan, 1957.

———. *Alexander Hamilton, The National Adventure 1788–1804.* New York: Macmillan, 1962.

———. *Heritage from Hamilton.* New York: Columbia University Press, 1957.

Pancake, John S. *Thomas Jefferson and Alexander Hamilton.* Woodbury, NY: Barrons, 1974.

Rossiter, Clinton. *Alexander Hamilton and the Constitution.* New York: Harcourt Brace Jovanovich, 1964.

Chronology

Jan. 11, 1755	Born Alexander Hamilton on Caribbean island of Nevis
1766	Becomes apprentice clerk for Nicholas Cruger
1773	Moves to New York, enters King's College
1775	Defends Continental Congress in two lengthy essays; joins militia in New York City
1776	Appointed captain in Continental Army, fights in the Battle of Trenton
1777	Sees action in battles of Princeton and Morristown, appointed aide-de-camp to General Washington with rank of lieutenant colonel
1778	Drafts Washington's report to Congress on reorganization of the army; fights at Monmouth
1780	Marries Elizabeth Schuyler, daughter of a New York aristocrat
Oct. 1781	Commands artillery battalion at the Battle of Yorktown
1782	Begins private law practice in New York; selected as delegate to the Continental Congress; writes *Continentalist* essays
1784	Founds Bank of New York
1786	Calls for a convention to amend the Articles of Confederation
1787	Serves in New York State Assembly and as delegate to Constitutional Convention
1787–1788	Writes *Federalist* essays with James Madison and John Jay
1788	Leads struggle for the ratification of the Constitution
1789	Appointed secretary of the Treasury by George Washington
1790	Issues report on public credit and report on a national bank
1790–1792	Hamilton's feud with Thomas Jefferson leads to creation of United States's first political parties
1791	Issues report on manufacturers and on the U.S. mint
1794	Leads army that quells Whiskey Rebellion
Dec. 1, 1794	Resigns from office
1795	Pens articles defending Jay's Treaty
1796	Helps Washington write Farewell Address
1797	Publicly discloses his love affair with Maria Reynolds
1798	Appointed inspector general of the army
1800	Writes letter criticizing President John Adams
1801	Founds *New York Evening Post*; eldest son killed in duel
July 11, 1804	Mortally wounded in a duel with Aaron Burr in Weehawken, New Jersey

Index

Steven O'Brien has taught high-school social studies in Massachusetts for 15 years. He holds an M.A. in history from the University of Connecticut and a certificate of advanced study from Harvard University, where he is currently a teaching fellow and doctoral candidate. His writing has appeared in the *New York Times Magazine* and other publications.

Arthur M. Schlesinger, jr., taught history at Harvard for many years and is currently Albert Schweitzer Professor of the Humanities at City University of New York. He is the author of numerous highly praised works in American history and has twice been awarded the Pulitzer Prize. He served in the White House as special assistant to Presidents Kennedy and Johnson.

10/31/96